Quick

And

Delicious

A HEALTHY EXCHANGES® COOKBOOK

JoAnna M. Lund

HELPing Others HELP Themselves
the **Healthy Exchanges**® Way™

A Perigee Book

A Perigee Book
Published by The Berkley Publishing Group
A division of Penguin Group (USA) Inc.
375 Hudson Street
New York, New York 10014

For more information about Healthy Exchanges products, contact:
Healthy Exchanges, Inc.
P.O. Box 80
DeWitt, Iowa 52742-0080
(563) 659-8324
Fax: (563) 659-2126

Perigee Special Sales edition: August 2003
ISBN 0-399-52980-2

The Putnam Group (USA) Inc. World Wide Web site address is
http://www.penguin.com

Portions of this book previously published in When Every Minute Counts, copyright
© 1998 by Healthy Exchanges, Inc. and 30 Meals/30 Minutes, copyright © 1997
by Healthy Exchanges, Inc.

Printed in the United States of America

10   9   8   7   6   5   4   3   2   1

Before using the recipes and advice in this book, consult your physician or health-care
provider to be sure they are appropriate for you. The information in this book is not
intended to take the place of any medical advice. It reflects the author's experiences,
studies, research, and opinions regarding a healthy lifestyle. All material included in
this publication is believed to be accurate. The publisher assumes no responsibility for
any health, welfare, or subsequent damage that might be incurred from the use of these
materials.

Contents

No Time to Cook? There's Still Time to Eat Healthy! or "Healthy" in a Hurry

It's 5:00 P.M.—or, even worse, nearly 6:00—when you hurry into the house from a day of working, shopping, carpooling, running errands, *whatever*. Everyone wants to know: "What's for dinner?" Who could blame you for ordering pizza, or piling the kids into the car for a quick trip to the nearest fast-food restaurant?

That's okay for once in a while, but too often quick-and-easy food is hard both on your waistline and your pocketbook. You'd prefer to offer your family healthy, good-tasting food every day, but is there time in your busy life to do what it takes?

I'm here to tell you that there *is*. I know exactly how it feels to juggle work and school and family, and *still* manage to find time to prepare delicious meals as part of your busy schedule. I've done it, managed to lose 130 pounds along the way—and kept it off now for six years!

My own success, which made it possible for me to help so many others, came because I finally understood that healthy eating didn't require hours in the kitchen, a hefty bank account, or a personal chef. My philosophy soon became clear: "**If it takes longer to cook it than eat it, forget it!**"

I got tired of sweating for ages over a hot stove, then finding myself with a sinkful of dirty dishes five minutes after the food hit the table. There had to be a better way, and I was determined to find it. Working from my tiny test kitchen in DeWitt, Iowa, I figured out ways to make traditional family recipes healthy—and make them *fast*! Now that the food manufacturers have jumped onto the Health Wagon with us, we can select from the best-quality reduced-fat and low-sugar convenience foods, add just the right amounts of fresh fruits, vegetables, meats, and dairy products, and produce meals that taste as good as they look!

My "common folk" healthy recipes are always low in sugar and fat, prepared from ingredients found in any small-town market, and perfect for diabetics, heart patients, and anyone concerned about weight loss or lowering cholesterol. But the ones I've selected for this volume are my "quickest of the quick," and I promise you'll find lots of great ideas for feeding your family fast—and healthy too!

Jo Anna

Six Tips for Making

Quick Recipes

Even Quicker

1. Purchase prechopped vegetables. Yes, already chopped fresh broccoli may cost you more, but you have *no* waste and save valuable time because you don't have to chop it yourself.

2. When cooking rice or pasta, always plan to cook extra and freeze the leftovers in two-cup portions. Then, whenever you need cooked macaroni for a quick main dish, all you have to do is thaw it in the microwave while you are browning the meat in a skillet.

3. When chopping onions or green peppers, chop several at once and freeze in half-cup portions. Frozen chopped fresh vegetables thaw in moments when browned with meat. (Take advantage of seasonal sales on produce or late-day specials at farm stands. If red peppers are usually $3.99 per pound and you spot them at half price, buy a bundle—then chop and freeze!)

4. Hard-boil six eggs at the same time. When they are cooled, mark each egg with a big **H** using a marker and store them unpeeled in an egg carton in the refrigerator. Then, when you want to add an egg to a salad, all you have to do is peel and chop.

5. Anytime roast chicken, turkey, pork, or beef is needed, simply purchase a lean chunk from the deli section of your grocery. When a recipe calls for cooked meat, dice as much as you need *right then*. You save roasting time, and you'll have no bones or fatty sections to cut off or throw away.

6. Kitchen shears are wonderful for cutting up canned tomatoes, peaches, or any whole fruit or vegetable in a can. Just snip "whatever" right in the can, then add it to your recipe. No bowl or countertop to clean, either!

JoAnna M. Lund

and Healthy Exchanges

Food is the first invited guest to every special occasion in every family's memory scrapbook. From baptism to graduation, from weddings to wakes, food brings us together.

It wasn't always that way at our house. I used to eat alone, even when my family was there, because while they were dining on real food, I was always nibbling at whatever my newest diet called for. In fact, for twenty-eight years I called myself the diet queen of DeWitt, Iowa.

I tried every diet I ever heard of, every one I could afford, and every one that found its way to my small town in eastern Iowa. I was willing to try anything that promised to "melt off the pounds," determined to deprive my body in every possible way in order to become thin at last.

I sent away for expensive "miracle" diet pills. I starved myself on the Cambridge Diet and the Bahama Diet. I gobbled Ayds diet candies, took thyroid pills, fiber pills, prescription and over-the-counter diet pills. I went to endless weight-loss support group meetings—but I somehow managed to turn healthy programs such as Overeaters Anonymous, Weight Watchers, and TOPS into unhealthy diets . . . diets I could never follow for more than a few months.

I was determined to discover something that worked long-term, but each new failure increased my desperation that I'd never find it.

I ate strange concoctions and rubbed on even stranger potions. I tried liquid diets like Slimfast and Metrecal. I agreed to be hypnotized. I tried reflexology and even had an acupuncture device stuck in my ear!

Does my story sound a lot like yours? I'm not surprised. No wonder the weight-loss business is a billion-dollar industry!

Every new thing I tried seemed to work—at least at first. And losing that first five or ten pounds would get me so excited, I'd believe that this new miracle diet would, finally, get my weight off for keeps.

Inevitably, though, the initial excitement wore off. The diet's routine and boredom set in, and I quit. I shoved the pills to the back of the medicine chest;

pushed the cans of powdered shake mix to the rear of the kitchen cabinets; slid all the program materials out of sight under my bed; and once more I felt like a failure.

Like most dieters, I quickly gained back the weight I'd lost each time, along with a few extra "souvenir" pounds that seemed always to settle around my hips. I'd done the diet-lose-weight-gain-it-all-back "yo-yo" on the average of once a year. It's no exaggeration to say that over the years I've lost 1,000 pounds—and gained back 1,150 pounds.

Finally, at the age of 46 I weighed more than I'd ever imagined possible. I'd stopped believing that any diet could work for me. I drowned my sorrows in sacks of cake donuts and wondered if I'd live long enough to watch my grandchildren grow up.

Something had to change.

I had to change.

Finally, I did.

I'm just over 50 now—and I'm 130 pounds less than my all-time high of close to 300 pounds. I've kept the weight off for more than six years. I'd like to lose another ten pounds, but I'm not obsessed about it. If it takes me two or three years to accomplish it, that's okay.

What I *do* care about is never saying hello again to any of those unwanted pounds I said good-bye to!

How did I jump off the roller coaster I was on? For one thing, I finally stopped looking to food to solve my emotional problems. But what really shook me up—and got me started on the path that changed my life—was Operation Desert Storm in early 1991. I sent three children off to the Persian Gulf War—my son-in-law, Matt, a medic in Special Forces; my daughter, Becky, a full-time college student and member of a medical unit in the Army Reserve; and my son, James, a member of the Inactive Army Reserve reactivated as a chemicals expert.

Somehow, knowing that my children were putting their lives on the line got me thinking about my own mortality—and I knew in my heart the last thing they needed while they were overseas was to get a letter from home saying that their mother was ill because of a food-related problem.

The day I drove the third child to the airport to leave for Saudi Arabia, something happened to me that would change my life for the better—and forever. I stopped praying my constant prayer as a professional dieter, which was simply "Please, God, let me lose ten pounds by Friday." Instead, I began praying, "God, please help me not to be a burden to my kids and my family." I quit praying for what I wanted and started praying for what I needed—and in the process my prayers were answered. I couldn't keep the kids safe—that was out of my hands— but I could try to get healthier to better handle the stress of it. It was the least I could do on the home front.

That quiet prayer was the beginning of the new JoAnna Lund. My initial goal was not to lose weight or create healthy recipes. I only wanted to become healthier for my kids, my husband, and myself.

Each of my children returned safely from the Persian Gulf War. But something didn't come back—the 130 extra pounds I'd been lugging around for far too long. I'd finally accepted the truth after all those agonizing years of suffering through on-again, off-again dieting.

There are no "magic" cures in life.

No "magic" potion, pill, or diet will make unwanted pounds disappear.

I found something better than magic, if you can believe it. When I turned my weight and health dilemma over to God for guidance, a new JoAnna Lund and Healthy Exchanges were born.

I discovered a new way to live my life—and uncovered an unexpected talent for creating easy "common folk" healthy recipes, and sharing my commonsense approach to healthy living. I learned that I could motivate others to change their lives and adopt a positive outlook. I began publishing cookbooks and a monthly food newsletter, and speaking to groups all over the country.

I like to say, *"When life handed me a lemon, not only did I make healthy, tasty lemonade, I wrote the recipe down!"*

What I finally found was not a quick fix or a short-term diet, but a great way to live well for a lifetime.

I want to share it with you.

Healthy Exchanges®

Weight Loss

Choices™/Exchanges

If you've ever been on one of the national weight-loss programs like Weight Watchers or Diet Center, you've already been introduced to the concept of measured portions of different food groups that make up your daily food plan. If you are not familiar with such a system of weight-loss choices or exchanges, here's a brief explanation. (If you want or need more detailed information, you can write to the American Dietetic Association or the American Diabetes Association for comprehensive explanations.)

The idea of food exchanges is to divide foods into basic food groups. The foods in each group are measured in servings that have comparable values. These groups include Proteins/Meats, Breads/Starches, Vegetables, Fats, Fruits, Skim Milk, Free Foods, and Optional Calories.

Each choice or exchange included in a particular group has about the same number of calories and a similar carbohydrate, protein, and fat content as the other foods in that group. Because any food on a particular list can be "exchanged" for any other food in that group, it makes sense to call the food groups *exchanges* or *choices*.

I like to think we are also "exchanging" bad habits and food choices for good ones!

By using Weight Loss Choices™ or exchanges you can choose from a variety of foods without having to calculate the nutrient value of each one. This makes it easier to include a wide variety of foods in your daily menus and gives you the opportunity to tailor your choices to your unique appetite.

If you want to lose weight, you should consult your physician or other weight-control expert regarding the number of servings that would be best for you from each food group. Since men generally require more calories than women, and since the requirements for growing children and teenagers differ from those for adults, the right number of exchanges for any one person is a personal decision. I have included a suggested plan of weight-loss choices in the pages following the exchange lists. It's a program I used to lose 130 pounds, and it's the one I still follow today.

(If you are a diabetic or have been diagnosed with heart problems, it is best to meet with your physician before using this or any other food program or recipe collection.)

Food Group Weight Loss Choices™/Exchanges

Not all food group exchanges are alike. The ones that follow are for anyone who's interested in weight loss or maintenance. Diabetic exchanges are calculated by the American Diabetic Association, and information about them is provided in *The Diabetic's Healthy Exchanges Cookbook* (Perigee Books).

Every Healthy Exchanges recipe provides calculations in three ways:

- Weight Loss Choices/Exchanges

- Calories, Fat, Protein, Carbohydrates, and Fiber Grams, and Sodium in milligrams

- Diabetic Exchanges calculated for me by a Registered Dietitian

Healthy Exchanges recipes can help you eat well and recover your health, whatever your health concerns may be. Please take a few minutes to review the exchange lists and the suggestions that follow on how to count them. You have lots of great eating in store for you!

Proteins

Meat, poultry, seafood, eggs, cheese, and legumes. One exchange of Protein is approximately 60 calories. Examples of one Protein choice or exchange:

1 ounce cooked weight of lean meat, poultry, or seafood
2 ounces white fish
1½ ounces 97% fat-free ham
1 egg (limit to no more than 4 per week)
¼ cup egg substitute
3 egg whites

¾ ounce reduced-fat cheese
½ cup fat-free cottage cheese
2 ounces cooked or ¾ ounce uncooked dry beans
1 tablespoon peanut butter (also count 1 fat exchange)

Breads

Breads, crackers, cereals, grains, and starchy vegetables. One exchange of Bread is approximately 80 calories. Examples of 1 Bread choice or exchange:

1 slice bread or 2 slices reduced-calorie bread (40 calories or less)
1 roll, any type (1 ounce)
½ cup cooked pasta or ¾ ounce uncooked (scant ½ cup)
½ cup cooked rice or 1 ounce uncooked (⅓ cup)
3 tablespoons flour
¾ ounce cold cereal
½ cup cooked hot cereal or ¾ ounce uncooked (2 tablespoons)
½ cup corn (kernels or cream-style) or peas
4 ounces white potato, cooked, or 5 ounces uncooked
3 ounces sweet potato, cooked, or 4 ounces uncooked
3 cups air-popped popcorn
7 fat-free crackers (¾ ounce)
3 (2½-inch squares) graham crackers
2 (¾-ounce) rice cakes or 6 mini
1 tortilla, any type (6-inch diameter)

Fruits

All fruits and fruit juices. One exchange of Fruit is approximately 60 calories. Examples of one Fruit choice or exchange:

1 small apple or ½ cup slices
1 small orange
½ medium banana
¾ cup berries (except strawberries and cranberries)
1 cup strawberries or cranberries
½ cup canned fruit, packed in fruit juice or rinsed well
2 tablespoons raisins
1 tablespoon spreadable fruit spread
½ cup apple juice (4 fluid ounces)
½ cup orange juice (4 fluid ounces)
½ cup applesauce

Skim Milk

Milk, buttermilk, and yogurt. One exchange of Skim Milk is approximately 90 calories. Examples of one Skim Milk choice or exchange:

1 cup skim milk
½ cup evaporated skim milk
1 cup low-fat buttermilk
¾ cup plain fat-free yogurt
⅓ cup nonfat dry milk powder

Vegetables

All fresh, canned, or frozen vegetables other than the starchy vegetables. One exchange of Vegetable is approximately 30 calories. Examples of one Vegetable choice or exchange:

½ cup vegetable
¼ cup tomato sauce
1 medium fresh tomato
½ cup vegetable juice

Fats

Margarine, mayonnaise, vegetable oils, salad dressings, olives, and nuts. One exchange of fat is approximately 40 calories. Examples of one Fat choice or exchange:

1 teaspoon margarine or 2 teaspoons reduced-calorie margarine
1 teaspoon butter
1 teaspoon vegetable oil
1 teaspoon mayonnaise or 2 teaspoons reduced-calorie mayonnaise
1 teaspoon peanut butter
1 ounce olives
¼ ounce pecans or walnuts

Free Foods

Foods that do not provide nutritional value but are used to enhance the taste of foods are included in the Free Foods group. Examples of these are spices, herbs, extracts, vinegar, lemon juice, mustard, Worcestershire sauce, and soy sauce. Cooking sprays and artificial sweeteners used in moderation are also included in this group. However, you'll see that I include the caloric value of artificial sweeteners in the Optional Calories of the recipes.

You may occasionally see a recipe that lists "free food" as part of the portion. According to the published exchange lists, a free food contains fewer than 20 calories per serving. Two or three servings per day of free foods/drinks are usually allowed in a meal plan.

Optional Calories

Foods that do not fit into any other group but are used in moderation in recipes are included in Optional Calories. Foods that are counted in this way include sugar-free gelatin and puddings, fat-free mayonnaise and dressings, reduced-calorie whipped toppings, reduced-calorie syrups and jams, chocolate chips, coconut, and canned broth.

Sliders™

These are 80 Optional Calorie increments that do not fit into any particular category. You can choose which food group to *slide* these into. It is wise to limit this selection to approximately three to four per day to ensure the best possible nutrition for your body while still enjoying an occasional treat.

Sliders™ may be used in either of the following ways:

1. If you have consumed all your Protein, Bread, Fruit, or Skim Milk Weight Loss Choices for the day, and you want to eat additional foods from those food groups, you simply use a Slider. It's what I call "healthy horse trading." Remember that Sliders may not be traded for choices in the Vegetables or Fats food groups.

2. Sliders may also be deducted from your Optional Calories for the day or week. ¼ Slider equals 20 Optional Calories; ½ Slider equals 40 Optional Calories; ¾ Slider equals 60 Optional Calories; and 1 Slider equals 80 Optional Calories.

Healthy Exchanges® Weight Loss Choices™

My original Healthy Exchanges program of Weight Loss Choices™ was based on an average daily total of 1,400 to 1,600 calories per day. That was what I determined was right for my needs, and for those of most women. Because men require additional calories (about 1,600 to 1,900), here are my suggested plans for women and men. (*If you require more or fewer calories, please revise this plan to meet your individual needs.*)

Each day, women should plan to eat:

2 Skim Milk servings, 90 calories each
2 Fat servings, 40 calories each

3 Fruit servings, 60 calories each
4 Vegetable servings or more, 30 calories each
5 Protein servings, 60 calories each
5 Bread servings, 80 calories each

Each day, men should plan to eat:

2 Skim Milk servings, 90 calories each
4 Fat servings, 40 calories each
3 Fruit servings, 60 calories each
4 Vegetable servings or more, 30 calories each
6 Protein servings, 60 calories each
7 Bread servings, 80 calories each

Young people should follow the program for men but add 1 Skim Milk serving for a total of 3 servings.

You may also choose to add up to 100 Optional Calories per day, and up to 21 to 28 Sliders per week at 80 calories each. If you choose to include more Sliders in your daily or weekly totals, deduct those 80 calories from your Optional Calorie "bank."

A word about **Sliders™:** These are to be counted toward your totals after you have used your allotment of choices of Skim Milk, Protein, Bread, and Fruit for the day. By "sliding" an additional choice into one of these groups, you can meet your individual needs for that day. Sliders are especially helpful when traveling, stressed-out, eating out, or for special events. I often use mine so I can enjoy my favorite Healthy Exchanges desserts. Vegetables are not to be counted as Sliders. Enjoy as many Vegetable choices as you need to feel satisfied. Because we want to limit our fat intake to moderate amounts, additional Fat choices should not be counted as Sliders. If you choose to include more fat on an *occasional* basis, count the extra choices as Optional Calories.

Keep a daily food diary of your Weight Loss Choices, checking off what you eat as you go. If, at the end of the day, your required selections are not 100 percent accounted for, but you have done the best you can, go to bed with a clear conscience. There will be days when you have ¼ Fruit or ½ Bread left over. What are you going to do—eat two slices of an orange or half a slice of bread and throw the rest out? I always say that "nothing in life comes out exact." Just do the best you can . . . *the best you can.*

Try to drink at least eight 8-ounce glasses of water a day. Water truly is the "nectar" of good health.

As a little added insurance, I take a multivitamin each day. It's not essential, but if my day's worth of well-planned meals "bites the dust" when unexpected events intrude on my regular routine, my body still gets its vital nutrients.

The calories listed in each group of choices are averages. Some choices within each group may be higher or lower, so it's important to select a variety of different foods instead of eating the same three or four all the time.

Use your Optional Calories! They are what I call "life's little extras." They make all the difference in how you enjoy your food and appreciate the variety available to you. Yes, we can get by without them, but do you really want to? Keep in mind that you should be using all your daily Weight Loss Choices first to ensure you are getting the basics of good nutrition. But I guarantee that Optional Calories will keep you from feeling deprived—and help you reach your weight-loss goals.

Sodium, Fat, Cholesterol, and Processed Foods

Are Healthy Exchanges ingredients really healthy? When I first created Healthy Exchanges, many people asked about sodium, about whether it was necessary to calculate the percentage of fat, saturated fat, and cholesterol in a healthy diet, and about my use of processed foods in many recipes. I researched these questions as I was developing my program, so you can feel confident about using the recipes and food plan.

Sodium

Most people consume more sodium than their bodies need. The American Heart Association and the American Diabetes Association recommend limiting daily sodium intake to no more than 3,000 milligrams per day. If your doctor suggests you limit your sodium even more, then *you really must read labels.*

Sodium is an essential nutrient and should not be completely eliminated. It helps to regulate blood volume and is needed for normal daily muscle and nerve functions. Most of us, however, have no trouble getting "all we need" and then some.

As with everything else, moderation is my approach. I rarely ever have salt in my list as an added ingredient. But if you're especially sodium-sensitive, make the right choices for you—and save high-sodium foods such as sauerkraut for an occasional treat.

I use lots of spices to enhance flavors, so you won't notice the absence of salt. In the few cases where it is used, salt is vital for the success of the recipe, so please don't omit it.

When I do use an ingredient high in sodium, I try to compensate by using low-sodium products in the remainder of the recipe. Many fat-free products are a little higher in sodium to make up for any loss of flavor that disappeared along with the fat. But when I take advantage of these fat-free, higher-sodium products, I stretch that ingredient within the recipe, lowering the amount of sodium per serving. A good example is my use of fat-free and reduced-sodium canned soups. While the suggested number of servings per can is 2, I make sure my final creation serves at least 4 and sometimes 6. So the soup's sodium has been "watered down" from one-third to one-half of the original amount.

Even if you don't have to watch your sodium intake for medical reasons, using moderation is another "healthy exchange" to make on your own journey to good health.

Fat Percentages

We've been told that 30 percent is the magic number—that we should limit fat intake to 30 percent or less of our total calories. It's good advice, and I try to have a weekly average of 15 percent to 25 percent myself. I believe any less than 15 percent is really just another restrictive diet that won't last. And more than 25 percent on a regular basis is too much of a good thing.

When I started listing fat grams along with calories in my recipes, I was tempted to include the percentage of calories from fat. After all, in the vast majority of my recipes, that percentage is well below 30 percent This even includes my pie recipes that allow you a realistic serving instead of many "diet" recipes that tell you a serving is one-twelfth of a pie.

Figuring fat grams is easy enough. Each gram of fat equals 9 calories. Multiply fat grams by 9, then divide that number by the total calories to get the percentage of calories from fat.

So why don't I do it? After consulting four registered dietitians for advice, I decided to omit this information. They felt that it's too easy for people to become obsessed by that 30 percent figure, which is after all supposed to be a percentage of total calories over the course of a day or a week. We mustn't feel we can't include a healthy ingredient such as pecans or olives in one recipe just because, on its own, it has more than 30 percent of its calories from fat.

An example of this would be a casserole made with 90 percent lean red meat. Most of us benefit from eating red meat in moderation, as it provides iron and niacin in our diets, and it also makes life more enjoyable for us and those who eat with us. If we *only* look at the percentage of calories from fat in a serving of this one dish, which might be as high as 40 to 45 percent, we might choose not to include this recipe in our weekly food plan.

The dietitians suggested that it's important to consider the total picture when making such decisions. As long as your overall food plan keeps fat calories to 30 percent, it's all right to enjoy an occasional dish that is somewhat higher in fat content. Healthy foods I include in **MODERATION** include 90 percent lean red meat, olives, and nuts. I don't eat these foods every day, and you may not either. But occasionally, in a good recipe, they make all the difference in the world between just getting by (deprivation) and truly enjoying your food.

Remember, the goal is eating in a healthy way so you can enjoy and live well the rest of your life.

Saturated Fats and Cholesterol

You'll see that I don't provide calculations for saturated fats or cholesterol amounts in my recipes. It's for the simple and yet not so simple reason that accurate, up-to-date, brand-specific information can be difficult to obtain from food manufacturers, especially since the way in which they produce food keeps changing rapidly. But once more I've consulted with Registered Dietitians and other professionals and found that, because I use only a few products that are high in saturated fat, and use them in such limited quantities, my recipes are suitable for patients concerned about controlling or lowering cholesterol. You'll also find that whenever I do use one of these ingredients *in moderation*, everything else in the recipe, and in the meals my family and I enjoy, is low in fat.

Processed Foods

Just what *is* processed food, anyway? What do I mean by the term "processed food," and why do I use them when the "purest" recipe developers in Recipe Land consider them "pedestrian" and won't ever use something from a box, container, or can? A letter I received and a passing statement from a stranger made me reflect on what I mean when I refer to processed foods, and helped me reaffirm why I use them in my "common folk" healthy recipes.

If you are like the vast millions who agree with me, then I'm not sharing anything new with you. And if you happen to disagree, that's okay, too. After all, this is America, the Land of the Free. We are blessed to live in a great nation where we can all believe what we want about anything.

A few months go, a woman sent me several articles from various "whole food" publications and wrote that she was wary of processed foods, and wondered why I used them in my recipes. She then scribbled on the bottom of her note, "Just how healthy *is* Healthy Exchanges?" Then, a few weeks later, during a chance visit at a public food event with a very pleasant woman, I was struck by how we all have our own definitions of what processed foods are. She shared with me, in a somewhat self-righteous manner, that she *never* uses processed foods. She only cooked with fresh fruits and vegetables, she told me. Then later she said that she used canned reduced-fat soups all the time! Was her definition different than mine, I wondered? Soup in a can, whether it's reduced in fat or not, still meets my definition of a processed food.

So I got out a copy of my book *HELP: Healthy Exchanges Lifetime Plan*, and reread what I had written back then about processed foods. Nothing in my definition had changed since I wrote that section. I still believe that healthy processed foods, such as canned soups, prepared piecrusts, sugar-free instant puddings, nonfat sour cream, and frozen whipped topping, when used properly, all have a place as ingredients in healthy recipes.

I never use an ingredient that hasn't been approved by either the American Diabetic Association, the American Dietetic Association, or the American Heart Association. Whenever I'm in doubt, I send for their position papers, then ask knowledgeable registered dietitians to explain those papers to me in "street language." I've been assured by all of them that the sugar- and fat-free products I use in my recipes are indeed safe.

If you don't agree, nothing I can say or write will convince you otherwise. But, if you've been using the healthy processed foods and have been concerned about the almost daily hoopla you hear about yet another product that's about the doom of all of us, then just stay with reason. For every product on the grocery shelves, there are those who want you to buy it and there are those who don't, *because they want you to buy their products instead*. So we have to learn to sift the fact from the fiction. Let's take sugar substitutes, for example. In making our own evaluations, we should toss out any information provided by the sugar substitute manufacturers, because they have a vested interest in our buying their products. Likewise, we should toss out any information provided by the sugar industry, because they have a vested interest in our not buying sugar substitutes. Then, if you aren't sure if you can really trust the government or any of its agencies, toss out their data, too. That leaves the three associations I mentioned above. Do you think any of them would say a product is safe if it isn't? Or say a product isn't safe when it is? They have nothing to gain or lose, *other than their integrity*, if they intentionally try to mislead us. That's why I only go to these associations for information concerning healthy processed foods.

I certainly don't recommend that everything we eat comes from a can, box, or jar. I think the best of all possible worlds is to start with the basics: grains such as rice, pasta, or corn. Then, for example, add some raw vegetables and extra-lean meat such as poultry, fish, beef, or pork. Stir in some healthy canned soup or tomato sauce, and you'll end up with something that is not only healthy but tastes so good, everyone from toddlers to great-grandparents will want to eat it!

I've never been in favor of spraying everything we eat with chemicals and I don't believe that all our foods should come out of packages. But I do think we should use the best available healthy processed foods to make cooking easier and food taste better. I take advantage of the good-tasting low-fat and low-sugar products found in any grocery store. My recipes are created for busy people like me, people who want to eat healthily and economically but who still want the food to satisfy their taste buds. I don't expect anyone to visit out-of-the-way health food stores or find the time to cook beans from scratch—*because I don't!* Most of you can't grow fresh food in the backyard and many of you may not have access to farmers' markets or large supermarkets. I want to help you figure out realistic ways to make healthy eating a reality *wherever you live*, or you will not stick to a healthy lifestyle for long.

So if you've been swayed (by individuals or companies with vested interests or hidden agendas) into thinking that all processed foods are bad for you, you may want to reconsider your position. Or if you've been fooling yourself into believing that you *never* use processed foods but regularly reach for that healthy canned soup, stop playing games with yourself—you are using processed foods in a healthy way. And, if you're like me and use healthy processed foods in *moderation*, don't let anyone make you feel ashamed about including these products in your healthy lifestyle. Only *you* can decide what's best for *you* and your family's needs.

Part of living a healthy lifestyle is making those decisions and then getting on with life. Congratulations on choosing to live a healthy lifestyle, and let's celebrate together by sharing a piece of Healthy Exchanges pie that I've garnished with Cool Whip Lite!

JoAnna's Ten Commandments of Successful Cooking

A very important part of any journey is knowing where you are going and the best way to get there. If you plan and prepare before you start to cook, you should reach mealtime with foods to write home about!

1. **Read the entire recipe from start to finish** and be sure you understand the process involved. Check that you have all the equipment you will need *before* you begin.

2. **Check the ingredient list** and be sure you have *everything* and in the amounts required. Keep cooking sprays handy—while they're not listed as ingredients, I use them all the time (just a quick squirt!).

3. **Set out *all*** the ingredients and equipment needed to prepare the recipe on the counter near you *before* you start. Remember that old saying, *A stitch in time saves nine?* It applies in the kitchen, too.

4. **Do as much advance preparation as possible** before actually cooking. Chop, cut, grate, or whatever is needed to prepare the ingredients and have them ready before you start to mix. Turn the oven on at least ten minutes before putting food in to bake, to allow the oven to preheat to the proper temperature.

5. **Use a kitchen timer** to tell you when the cooking or baking time is up. Because stove temperatures vary slightly by manufacturer, you may want to set your timer for five minutes less than the suggested time just to prevent overcooking. Check the progress of your dish at that time, then decide if you need the additional minutes or not.

6. **Measure carefully.** Use glass measures for liquids and metal or plastic cups for dry ingredients. My recipes are based on standard measurements. Unless I tell you it's a scant or full cup, measure the cup level.

7. **For best results, follow the recipe instructions exactly.** Feel free to substitute ingredients that *don't tamper* with the basic chemistry of the recipe, but be sure to leave key ingredients alone. For example, you could substitute sugar-free instant chocolate pudding for sugar-free butterscotch instant pudding, but if you used a six-serving package when a four-serving package was listed in the ingredients, or you used instant when cook-and-serve is required, you won't get the right result.

8. **Clean up as you go.** It is much easier to wash a few items at a time than to face a whole counter of dirty dishes later. The same is true for spills on the counter or floor.

9. **Be careful about doubling or halving a recipe.** Though many recipes can be altered successfully to serve more or fewer people, *many cannot.* This is especially true when it comes to spices and liquids. If you try to double a recipe that calls for 1 teaspoon pumpkin-pie spice, for example, and you double the spice, you may end up with a too-spicy taste. I usually suggest increasing spices or liquid by 1½ times when doubling a recipe. If it tastes a little bland to you, you can increase the spice to 1¾ times the original amount the next time you prepare the dish. Remember: You can always add more, but you can't take it out after it's stirred in.

   The same is true with liquid ingredients. If you wanted to **triple** a recipe like my **Easy Italian Meat Loaf** because you were planning to serve a crowd, you might think you should use three times as much of every ingredient. Don't, or you could end up with Italiano Meat Loaf Soup! The original recipe calls for 1¾ cups of chunky tomato sauce, so I'd suggest using 3½ cups when you **triple** the recipe (or 2¾ cups if you **double** it). You'll still have a good-tasting dish that won't run all over the plate.

10. **Write your reactions next to each recipe once you've served it.** Yes, that's right, I'm giving you permission to write in this book. It's yours, after all. Ask yourself: Did everyone like it? Did you have to add another half teaspoon of chili seasoning to please your family, who like to live on the spicier side of the street? You may even want to rate the recipe on a scale of 1★ to 4★, depending on what you thought of it. (Four stars would be the top rating—and I hope you'll feel that way about many of my recipes.) Jotting down your comments while they are fresh in your mind will help you personalize the recipe to your own taste the next time you prepare it.

My Best Healthy Exchanges Tips and Tidbits

Measurements, General Cooking Tips, and Basic Ingredients

The word *moderation* best describes **my use of fats, sugar substitutes,** and **sodium** in these recipes. Wherever possible, I've used cooking spray for sautéing and for browning meats and vegetables. I also use reduced-calorie margarine and no-fat mayonnaise and salad dressings. Lean ground turkey *or* ground beef can be used in the recipes. Just be sure whatever you choose is at least *90 percent lean*.

I've also included **small amounts of sugar and brown sugar substitutes as the sweetening agent** in many of the recipes. I don't drink a hundred cans of soda a day or eat enough artificially sweetened foods in a 24-hour time period to be troubled by sugar substitutes. But if this is a concern of yours and you *do not* need to watch your sugar intake, you can always replace the sugar substitutes with processed sugar and the sugar-free products with regular ones.

I created my recipes knowing they would also be used by hypoglycemics, diabetics, and those concerned about triglycerides. If you choose to use sugar instead, be sure to count the additional calories.

A word of caution when cooking with **sugar substitutes**: Use **saccharin**-based sweeteners when **heating or baking**. In recipes that **don't require heat, aspartame** (known as NutraSweet) works well in uncooked dishes but leaves an aftertaste in baked products.

I'm often asked why I use an **8-by-8-inch baking dish** in my recipes. It's for portion control. If the recipe says it serves 4, just cut down the center, turn the dish, and cut again. Like magic, there's your serving. Also, if this is the only recipe you are preparing requiring an oven, the square dish fits into a tabletop toaster oven easily and energy can be conserved.

To make life even easier, **whenever a recipe calls for ounce measurements** (other than raw meats) I've included the closest cup equivalent. I need to use my scale daily when creating recipes, so I've measured for you at the same time.

Most of the recipes are for **4 to 6 servings**. If you don't have that many to feed, do what I do: freeze individual portions. Then all you have to do is choose something from the freezer and take it to work for lunch or have your evening meals prepared in advance for the week. In this way, I always have something on hand that is both good to eat and good for me.

Unless a recipe includes hard-boiled eggs, cream cheese, mayonnaise, or a raw vegetable or fruit, **the leftovers should freeze well**. (I've marked recipes that freeze well with the symbol of a **snowflake ❄**.) This includes most of the cream pies. Divide any recipe up into individual servings and freeze for your own "TV" dinners.

Another good idea is **cutting leftover pie into individual pieces and freezing each one separately** in a small Ziploc freezer bag. Then the next time you want to thaw a piece of pie for yourself, you don't have to thaw the whole pie. It's great this way for brown-bag lunches, too. Just pull a piece out of the freezer on your way to work and by lunchtime you will have a wonderful dessert waiting for you.

Unless I specify **"covered" for simmering or baking**, prepare my recipes **uncovered**. Occasionally you will read a recipe that asks you to cover a dish for a time, then to uncover, so read the directions carefully to avoid confusion—and to get the best results.

Low-fat cooking spray is another blessing in a Healthy Exchanges kitchen. It's currently available in three flavors . . .

- •**OLIVE-OIL FLAVORED** when cooking Mexican, Italian, or Greek dishes

- •**BUTTER FLAVORED** when the hint of butter is desired

- •**REGULAR** for everything else.

A quick spray of butter flavored makes air-popped popcorn a low-fat taste treat, or try it as a butter substitute on steaming hot corn on the cob. One light spray of the skillet when browning meat will convince you that you're using "old-fashioned fat," and a quick coating of the casserole dish before you add the ingredients will make serving easier and cleanup quicker.

I use reduced-sodium **canned chicken broth** in place of dry bouillon to lower the sodium content. The intended flavor is still present in the prepared dish. As a reduced-sodium beef broth is not currently available (at least not in DeWitt, Iowa), I use the canned regular beef broth. The sodium content is still lower than regular dry bouillon.

Whenever **cooked rice or pasta** is an ingredient, follow the package directions, but eliminate the salt and/or margarine called for. This helps lower the sodium and fat content. It tastes just fine; trust me on this.

Here's another tip: When **cooking rice or noodles**, why not cook extra "for the pot"? After you use what you need, store leftover rice in a covered container (where it will keep for a couple of days). With noodles like spaghetti or macaroni, first rinse and drain as usual, then measure out what you need. Put the leftovers in a bowl covered with water, then store in the refrigerator, covered, until they're needed. Then, measure out what you need, rinse and drain them, and they're ready to go.

Does your **pita bread** often tear before you can make a sandwich? Here's my tip to make them open easily: cut the bread in half, put the halves in the microwave for about 15 seconds, and they will open up by themselves. *Voilà!*

When **chunky salsa** is listed as an ingredient, I leave the degree of "heat" up to your personal taste. In our house, I'm considered a wimp. I go for the "mild" while Cliff prefers "extra-hot." How do we compromise? I prepare the recipe with mild salsa because he can always add a spoonful or two of the hotter version to his serving, but I can't enjoy the dish if it's too spicy for me.

Milk and Yogurt

Take it from me—nonfat dry milk powder is great! I *do not* use it for drinking, but I *do* use it for cooking. Three good reasons why:

(1) It is very **inexpensive**.

(2) It **does not sour** because you use it only as needed. Store the box in your refrigerator or freezer and it will keep almost forever.

(3) You can easily **add extra calcium** to just about any recipe without added liquid. I consider nonfat dry milk powder one of Mother Nature's modern-day miracles of convenience. But do purchase a good national name brand (I like Carnation), and keep it fresh by proper storage.

In many of my pies and puddings, I use nonfat dry milk powder and water instead of skim milk. Usually I call for ⅔ cup nonfat dry milk powder and 1¼ to 1½ cups water or liquid. This way I can get the nutrients of two cups of milk, but much less liquid, and the end result is much creamier. Also, the recipe sets up quicker, usually in 5 minutes or less. So if someone knocks at your door unexpectedly at mealtime, you can quickly throw a pie together and enjoy it minutes later.

You can make your own **"sour cream"** by combining ¾ cup plain fat-free yogurt with ⅓ cup nonfat dry milk powder. What you did by doing this is fourfold: 1) The dry milk stabilizes the yogurt and keeps the whey from separating. 2) The dry milk slightly helps to cut the tartness of the yogurt. 3) It's still virtually fat-free. 4) The calcium has been increased by 100 percent. Isn't it great how we can make that distant relative of sour cream a first kissin' cousin by adding the nonfat dry milk powder? Or, if you place 1 cup of plain fat-free yogurt in a sieve lined with a coffee filter, and place the sieve over a small bowl and refrigerate for about 6 hours, you will end up with a very good alternative for sour cream. To **stabilize yogurt** when cooking or baking with it, just add 1 teaspoon cornstarch to every ¾ cup yogurt.

If a recipe calls for **evaporated skim milk** and you don't have any in the cupboard, make your own. For every ½ cup evaporated skim milk needed, combine ⅓ cup nonfat dry milk powder and ½ cup water. Use as you would evaporated skim milk.

You can also make your own **sugar-free and fat-free sweetened condensed milk** at home. Combine 1⅓ cups nonfat dry milk powder and ½ cup cold water in a 2-cup glass measure. Cover and microwave on HIGH until mixture is hot but *not* boiling. Stir in ½ cup Sprinkle Sweet or Sugar Twin. Cover and refrigerate at least 4 hours. This mixture will keep for up to 2 weeks in the refrigerator. Use in just about any recipe that calls for sweetened condensed milk.

For any recipe that calls for **buttermilk**, you might want to try JO's Buttermilk: Blend one cup of water and ⅔ cup dry milk powder (the nutrients of two cups of skim milk). It'll be thicker than this mixed-up milk usually is, because it's doubled. Add 1 teaspoon white vinegar and stir, then let it sit for at least 10 minutes.

One of my subscribers was looking for a way to further restrict salt intake, and needed a substitute for **cream of mushroom soup**. For many of my recipes, I use Healthy Request Cream of Mushroom Soup, as it is a reduced-sodium product. The label suggests 2 servings per can, but I usually incorporate the soup into a recipe serving at least four. By doing this, I've reduced the sodium in the soup by half again.

But if you must restrict your sodium even more, try making my Healthy Exchanges **Creamy Mushroom Sauce**. Place 1½ cups evaporated skim milk and 3 tablespoons flour in a covered jar. Shake well and pour mixture into a medium saucepan sprayed with butter-flavored cooking spray. Add ½ cup canned sliced mushrooms, rinsed and drained. Cook over medium heat, stirring often, until mixture thickens. Add any seasonings of your choice. You can use this sauce in any recipe that calls for one 10¾-ounce can of cream of mushroom soup.

Why did I choose these proportions and ingredients?

- 1½ cups evaporated skim milk is the amount in one can.

- It's equal to three milk choices or exchanges.

- It's the perfect amount of liquid and flour for a medium cream sauce.

- 3 tablespoons flour is equal to one bread/starch choice or exchange.

- Any leftovers will reheat beautifully with a flour-based sauce, but not with a cornstarch base.

- The mushrooms are one vegetable choice or exchange.

- This sauce is virtually fat-free, sugar-free, and sodium-free.

Proteins

I use eggs in moderation. I enjoy the real thing on an average of three to four times a week. So, my recipes are calculated on using whole eggs. However, if you choose to use egg substitute in place of the egg, the finished product will turn out just fine and the fat grams per serving will be even lower than those listed.

If you like the look, taste, and feel of **hard-boiled eggs** in salads but haven't been using them because of the cholesterol in the yolk, I have a couple of alternatives for you. 1) Pour an 8-ounce carton of egg substitute into a medium skillet sprayed with cooking spray. Cover skillet tightly and cook over low heat until substitute is just set, about 10 minutes. Remove from heat and let set, still covered, for 10 minutes more. Uncover and cool completely. Chop set mixture. This will make about 1 cup of chopped egg. 2) Even easier is to hard-boil "real eggs," toss the yolk away, and chop the white. Either way, you don't deprive yourself of the pleasure of egg in your salad.

In most recipes calling for **egg substitutes**, you can use 2 egg whites in place of the equivalent of 1 egg substitute. Just break the eggs open and toss the yolks away. I can hear some of you already saying, "But that's wasteful!" Well, take a look at the price on the egg substitute package (which usually has the equivalent of 4 eggs in it), then look at the price of a dozen eggs, from which you'd get the equivalent of 6 egg substitutes. Now, what's wasteful about that?

Whenever I include **cooked chicken** in a recipe, I use roasted white meat without skin. Whenever I include **roast beef or pork** in a recipe, I use the loin cuts because they are much leaner. However, most of the time, I do my roasting of all these meats at the local deli. I just ask for a chunk of their lean roasted meat, 6 or 8 ounces, and ask them not to slice it. When I get home, I cube or dice the meat and am ready to use it in my recipe. The reason I do this is threefold: 1) I'm getting just the amount I need without leftovers; 2) I don't have the expense of heating the oven; and 3) I'm not throwing away the bone, gristle, and fat I'd be cutting away from the meat. Overall, it is probably cheaper to "roast" it the way I do.

Did you know that you can make an acceptable meat loaf without using egg for the binding? Just replace every egg with ¼ cup of liquid. You could use beef broth, tomato sauce, even applesauce, to name just a few. For a meat loaf to serve 6, I always use 1 pound of extra-lean ground beef or turkey, 6 tablespoons of dried fine bread crumbs, and ¼ cup of the liquid, plus anything else healthy that strikes my fancy at the time. I mix well and place the mixture in an 8-by-8-inch baking dish or 9-by-5-inch loaf pan sprayed with cooking spray. Bake uncovered at 350 degrees for 35 to 50 minutes (depending on the added ingredients). You will never miss the egg.

Any time you are **browning ground meat** for a casserole and want to get rid of almost all the excess fat, just place the uncooked meat loosely in a plastic colander. Set the colander in a glass pie plate. Place in microwave and cook on HIGH for 3 to 6 minutes (depending on the amount being browned), stirring often. Use as you would for any casserole. You can also chop up onions and brown them with the meat if you want.

Fruits and Vegetables

If you want to enjoy a **"fruit shake"** with some pizzazz, just combine soda water and unsweetened fruit juice in a blender. Add crushed ice. Blend on HIGH until thick. Refreshment without guilt.

You'll see that many recipes use ordinary **canned vegetables**. They're much cheaper than reduced-sodium versions, and once you rinse and drain them, the sodium is reduced anyway. I believe in saving money wherever possible so we can afford the best fat-free and sugar-free products as they come onto the market.

All three kinds of **vegetables—fresh, frozen, and canned—**have their place in a healthy diet. My husband, Cliff, hates the taste of frozen or fresh green beans, thinks the texture is all wrong, so I use canned green beans instead. In this case, canned vegetables have their proper place when I'm feeding my husband. If someone in your family has a similar concern, it's important to respond to it so everyone can be happy and enjoy the meal.

When I use **fruits or vegetables** like apples, cucumbers, and zucchini, I wash them really well and **leave the skin on**. It provides added color, fiber, and attractiveness to any dish. And, because I use processed flour in my cooking, I like to increase the fiber in my diet by eating my fruits and vegetables in their closest-to-natural state.

To help keep **fresh fruits and veggies fresh**, just give them a quick "shower" with lemon juice. The easiest way to do this is to pour purchased lemon juice into a kitchen spray bottle and store in the refrigerator. Then, every time you use fresh fruits or vegetables in a salad or dessert, simply give them a quick spray with your "lemon spritzer." You just might be amazed by how this little trick keeps your produce from turning brown so fast.

The next time you warm canned vegetables such as carrots or green beans, drain and heat the vegetables in $\frac{1}{4}$ cup beef or chicken broth. It gives a nice variation to an old standby. Here's a simple **white sauce** for vegetables and casseroles without using added fat that can be made by spraying a medium saucepan with butter-flavored cooking spray. Place $1\frac{1}{2}$ cups evaporated skim milk and 3 tablespoons flour in a covered jar. Shake well. Pour into sprayed saucepan and cook over medium heat until thick, stirring constantly. Add salt and pepper to taste. You can also add $\frac{1}{2}$ cup canned drained mushrooms and/or 3 ounces ($\frac{3}{4}$ cup) shredded reduced-fat cheese. Continue cooking until cheese melts.

Zip up canned or frozen green beans with **chunky salsa**: $\frac{1}{2}$ cup to 2 cups beans. Heat thoroughly. Chunky salsa also makes a wonderful dressing on lettuce salads. It only counts as a vegetable, so enjoy.

Another wonderful **South of the Border** dressing can be stirred up by using $\frac{1}{2}$ cup of chunky salsa and $\frac{1}{4}$ cup fat-free Ranch dressing. Cover and store in your refrigerator. Use as a dressing for salads or as a topping for baked potatoes.

For **gravy** with all the "old time" flavor but without the extra fat, try this almost effortless way to prepare it. (It's almost as easy as opening up a store-bought jar.) Pour the juice off your roasted meat, then set the roast aside to "rest" for about 20 minutes. Place the juice in an uncovered cake pan or other large flat pan (we want the large air surface to speed up the cooling process) and put in the freezer until the fat congeals on top and you can skim it off. Or, if you prefer, use a skimming pitcher purchased at your kitchen gadget store. Either way, measure about $1\frac{1}{2}$ cups skimmed broth and pour into a medium saucepan. Cook over medium heat until heated through, about 5 minutes. In a covered jar, combine $\frac{1}{2}$ cup water or cooled potato broth with 3 tablespoons flour. Shake well. Pour flour mixture into warmed juice. Combine well using a wire whisk. Continue cooking until gravy thickens, about 5 minutes. Season with salt and pepper to taste.

Why did I use flour instead of cornstarch? Because any leftovers will reheat nicely with the flour base and would not with a cornstarch base. Also, 3 tablespoons of flour works out to 1 Bread/Starch exchange. This virtually fat-free gravy makes about 2 cups, so you could spoon about $\frac{1}{2}$ cup gravy on your low-fat mashed potatoes and only have to count your gravy as $\frac{1}{4}$ Bread/Starch exchange.

Desserts

Thaw **lite whipped topping** in the refrigerator overnight. Never try to force the thawing by stirring or using a microwave to soften. Stirring it will remove the air from the topping that gives it the lightness and texture we want, and there's not enough fat in it to survive being heated.

How can I **frost an entire pie with just ½ cup of whipped topping?** First, don't use an inexpensive brand. I use Cool Whip Lite or La Creme Lite. Make sure the topping is fully thawed. Always spread from the center to the sides using a rubber spatula. This way, ½ cup topping will literally cover an entire pie. Remember, the operative word is *frost*, not pile the entire container on top of the pie!

For a special treat that tastes anything but "diet," try placing **spreadable fruit** in a container and microwave for about 15 seconds. Then pour the melted fruit spread over a serving of nonfat ice cream or frozen yogurt. One tablespoon of spreadable fruit is equal to 1 fruit serving. Some combinations to get you started are apricot over chocolate ice cream, strawberry over strawberry ice cream, or any flavor over vanilla.

Another way I use spreadable fruit is to make a delicious **topping for a cheesecake or angel food cake**. I take ½ cup of fruit and ½ cup Cool Whip Lite and blend the two together with a teaspoon of coconut extract.

Here's a really **good topping** for the fall of the year. Place 1½ cups unsweetened applesauce in a medium saucepan or 4-cup glass measure. Stir in 2 tablespoons raisins, 1 teaspoon apple pie spice, and 2 tablespoons Cary's Sugar Free Maple Syrup. Cook over medium heat on stove or process on HIGH in microwave until warm. Then spoon about ½ cup warm mixture over pancakes, French toast, or fat-free and sugar-free vanilla ice cream. It's as close as you will get to guilt-free apple pie!

A quick yet tasty way to prepare **strawberries for shortcake** is to place about ¾ cup sliced strawberries, 2 tablespoons Diet Mountain Dew, and sugar substitute to equal ¼ cup sugar in a blender container. Process on BLEND until mixture is smooth. Pour mixture into bowl. Add 1¼ cups sliced strawberries and mix well. Cover and refrigerate until ready to serve with shortcake.

The next time you are making treats for the family, try using **unsweetened applesauce** for some or all of the required oil in the recipe. For instance, if the recipe calls for ½ cup cooking oil, use up to the ½ cup in applesauce. It works and most people will not even notice the difference. It's great in purchased cake mixes, but so far I haven't been able to figure out a way to deep-fat fry with it!

Another trick I often use is to include tiny amounts of "real people" food, such as coconut, but extend the flavor by using extracts. Try it—you will be surprised by how little of the real thing you can use and still feel you are not being deprived.

If you are preparing a pie filling that has ample moisture, just line **graham crackers** in the bottom of a 9-by-9-inch cake pan. Pour the filling over the top of the crackers. Cover and refrigerate until the moisture has enough time to soften the crackers. Overnight is best. This eliminates the added **fats and sugars of a piecrust.**

When **stirring fat-free cream cheese to soften it**, use only a sturdy spoon, never an electric mixer. The speed of a mixer can cause the cream cheese to lose its texture and become watery.

Did you know you can make your own **fruit-flavored yogurt**? Mix 1 tablespoon of any flavor of spreadable fruit spread with ¾ cup plain yogurt. It's every bit as tasty and much cheaper. You can also make your own **lemon yogurt** by combining 3 cups plain fat-free yogurt with 1 tub Crystal Light lemonade powder. Mix well, cover, and store in refrigerator. I think you will be pleasantly surprised by the ease, cost, and flavor of this "made from scratch" calcium-rich treat. P.S.: You can make any flavor you like by using any of the Crystal Light mixes— Cranberry? Iced tea? You decide.

Sugar-free puddings and gelatins are important to many of my recipes, but if you prefer to avoid sugar substitutes, you could still prepare the recipes with regular puddings or gelatins. The calories would be higher, but you would still be cooking low-fat.

When a recipe calls for **chopped nuts** (and you only have whole ones), who wants to dirty the food processor just for a couple of tablespoons? You could try to chop them using your cutting board, but be prepared for bits and pieces to fly all over the kitchen. I use "Grandma's food processor." I use the biggest nuts I can find, put them in a small glass bowl, and chop them into chunks just the right size using a metal biscuit cutter.

If you have a **leftover muffin** and are looking for something a little different for breakfast, you can make a **"breakfast sundae."** Crumble the muffin into a cereal bowl. Sprinkle a serving of fresh fruit over it and top with a couple of tablespoons nonfat plain yogurt sweetened with sugar substitute and your choice of extract. The thought of it just might make you jump out of bed with a smile on your face. (Speaking of muffins, did you know that if you fill the unused muffin wells with water when baking muffins, you help ensure more even baking and protect the muffin pan at the same time?) Another muffin hint: Lightly spray the inside of paper baking cups with butter-flavored cooking spray before spooning the muffin batter into them. Then you won't end up with paper clinging to your fresh-baked muffins.

The secret of making **good meringues** without sugar is to use 1 tablespoon of Sprinkle Sweet or Sugar Twin for every egg white, and a small amount of extract. Use ½ to 1 teaspoon for the batch. Almond, vanilla, and coconut are all good choices. Use the same amount of cream of tartar you usually do. Bake the meringue in the same old way. Don't think you can't have meringue pies because you can't eat sugar. You can, if you do it my way. (Remember that egg whites whip up best at room temperature.)

Homemade or Store-Bought?

I've been asked which is better for you: homemade from scratch, or purchased foods. My answer is *both!* They each have a place in a healthy lifestyle, and what that place is has everything to do with you.

Take **piecrusts**, for instance. If you love spending your spare time in the kitchen preparing foods, and you're using low-fat, low-sugar, and reasonably low sodium ingredients, go for it! But if, like so many people, your time is limited and you've learned to read labels, you could be better off using purchased foods.

I know that when I prepare a pie (and I experiment with a couple of pies each week, because this is Cliff's favorite dessert) I use a purchased crust. Why? Mainly because I can't make a good-tasting piecrust that is lower in fat than the brands I use. Also, purchased piecrusts fit my rule of "If it takes longer to fix than to eat, forget it!"

I've checked the nutrient information for the purchased piecrusts against recipes for traditional and "diet" piecrusts, using my computer software program. The purchased crust calculated lower in both fat and calories! I have tried some low-fat and low-sugar recipes, but they just didn't spark my taste buds, or were so complicated you needed an engineering degree just to get the crust in the pie plate.

I'm very happy with the purchased piecrusts in my recipes, because the finished product rarely, if ever, has more than 30 percent of total calories coming from fats. I also believe that we have to prepare foods our families and friends will eat with us on a regular basis and not feel deprived, or we've wasted time, energy, and money.

I could use a purchased "lite" **pie filling**, but instead I make my own. Here I can save both fat and sugar, and still make the filling almost as fast as opening a can. The bottom line: Know what you have to spend when it comes to both time and fat/sugar calories, then make the best decision you can for you and your family. And don't go without an occasional piece of pie because you think it isn't *necessary.* A delicious pie prepared in a healthy way is one of the simple pleasures of life. It's a little thing, but it can make all the difference between just getting by with the bare minimum and living a full and healthy lifestyle.

Many people have experimented with my tip about **substituting applesauce and artificial sweetener for butter and sugar**, but what if you aren't satisfied with the result? One woman wrote to me about a recipe for her grandmother's cookies that called for 1 cup butter and 1½ cups sugar. Well, any recipe that depends on as much butter and sugar as this one does is generally not a good candidate for "healthy exchanges." The original recipe needed a large quantity of fat to produce a crisp cookie just like Grandma made.

Unsweetened applesauce can be used to substitute for vegetable oil with various degrees of success, but not to replace butter, lard, or margarine. If your recipe calls for ½ cup oil or less, and it's a quick bread, muffin, or bar cookie, it should work to replace the oil with applesauce. If the recipe calls for more than ½ cup oil, then experiment with half oil, half applesauce. You've still made the recipe healthier, even if you haven't removed all the oil from it.

Another rule for healthy substitution: Up to ½ cup sugar or less can be replaced by *an artificial sweetener that can withstand the heat of baking*, like Sugar Twin or Sprinkle Sweet. If it requires more than ½ cup sugar, cut the amount needed by 75 percent and use ½ cup sugar substitute and sugar for the rest. Other options: reduce the butter and sugar by 25 percent and see if the finished product still satisfies you in taste and appearance. Or, make the cookies just like Grandma did, realizing they are part of your family's holiday tradition. Enjoy a moderate serving of a couple of cookies once or twice during the season, and just forget about them the rest of the year.

I'm sure you'll add to this list of cooking tips as you begin preparing Healthy Exchanges recipes and discover how easy it can be to adapt your own favorite recipes using these ideas and your own common sense.

A Peek into
My Pantry and
My Favorite Brands

Everyone asks me what foods I keep on hand and what brands I use. There are lots of good products on the grocery shelves today—many more than we dreamed about even a year or two ago. And I can't wait to see what's out there twelve months from now. The following are my staples and, where appropriate, my favorites *at this time*. I feel these products are healthier, tastier, easy to get—and deliver the most flavor for the least amount of fat, sugar, or calories. If you find others you like as well *or better*, please use them. This is only a guide to make your grocery shopping and cooking easier.

Fat-free plain yogurt (*Yoplait or Dannon*)
Nonfat dry skim milk powder (*Carnation*)
Evaporated skim milk (*Carnation*)
Skim milk
Fat-free cottage cheese
Fat-free cream cheese (*Philadelphia*)
Fat-free mayonnaise (*Kraft*)
Fat-free salad dressings (*Kraft*)
Fat-free sour cream (*Land O Lakes*)
Reduced-calorie margarine (*Weight Watchers, Promise, or Smart Beat*)
Cooking spray:
    Olive-oil flavored and regular (*Pam*)
    Butter flavored for sautéing (*Weight Watchers*)
    Butter flavored for spritzing *after* cooking (*I Can't Believe It's Not Butter!*)
Vegetable oil (*Puritan Canola Oil*)
Reduced-calorie whipped topping (*Cool Whip Lite or Cool Whip Free*)

Sugar Substitute
 if no heating is involved (*Equal*)
 if heating is required
  white (*Sugar Twin or Sprinkle Sweet*)
  brown (*Brown Sugar Twin*)
Sugar-free gelatin and pudding mixes (*JELL-O*)
Baking mix (*Bisquick Reduced Fat*)
Pancake mix (*Aunt Jemima Reduced Calorie*)
Reduced-calorie pancake syrup (*Cary's Sugar Free*)
Parmesan cheese (*Kraft fat-free*)
Reduced-fat cheese (*Kraft ⅓ Less Fat*)
Shredded frozen potatoes (*Mr. Dell's*)
Spreadable fruit spread (*Knott's Berry Farm, Smucker's, or Welch's*)
Peanut butter (*Peter Pan reduced-fat, Jif reduced-fat, or Skippy reduced-fat*)
Chicken broth (*Healthy Request*)
Beef broth (*Swanson*)
Tomato sauce (*Hunt's—Chunky and Regular*)
Canned soups (*Healthy Request*)
Tomato juice (*Campbell's Reduced-Sodium*)
Ketchup (*Heinz Light Harvest or Healthy Choice*)
Purchased piecrust
 unbaked (*Pillsbury—from dairy case*)
 graham cracker, butter flavored, or chocolate flavored (*Keebler*)
Crescent rolls (*Pillsbury Reduced Fat*)
Pastrami and corned beef (*Carl Buddig Lean*)
Luncheon meats (*Healthy Choice or Oscar Mayer*)
Ham (*Dubuque 97% fat-free and reduced-sodium or Healthy Choice*)
Frankfurters and Kielbasa sausage (*Healthy Choice*)
Canned white chicken, packed in water (*Swanson*)
Canned tuna, packed in water (*Chicken of the Sea*)
90 to 95 percent lean ground turkey and beef
Soda crackers (*Nabisco Fat-Free*)
Reduced-calorie bread—40 calories per slice or less
Hamburger buns—80 calories each (*Less*)
Rice—instant, regular, brown, and wild
Instant potato flakes (*Betty Crocker Potato Buds*)
Noodles, spaghetti, and macaroni
Salsa (*Chi Chi's Mild Chunky*)
Pickle relish—dill, sweet, and hot dog
Mustard—Dijon, prepared, and spicy
Unsweetened apple juice

Unsweetened applesauce
Fruit—fresh, frozen (no sugar added), or canned in juice
Vegetables—fresh, frozen, or canned
Spices—JO's Spices
Lemon and lime juice (in small plastic fruit-shaped bottles found in produce section)
Instant fruit beverage mixes (*Crystal Light*)
Dry dairy beverage mixes (*Nestlé's Quik and Swiss Miss*)
"Ice Cream"—*Wells' Blue Bunny sugar- and fat-free*

The items on my shopping list are everyday foods found in just about any grocery store in America. But all are as low in fat, sugar, calories, and sodium as I can find—and that still taste good! I can make any recipe in my cookbooks and newsletters as long as I have my cupboards and refrigerator stocked with these items. Whenever I use the last of any one item, I just make sure I pick up another supply the next time I'm at the store.

If your grocer does not stock these items, why not ask if they can be ordered on a trial basis? If the store agrees to do so, be sure to tell your friends to stop by, so that sales are good enough to warrant restocking the new products. Competition for shelf space is fierce, so only products that sell well stay around.

Shopping The
Healthy Exchanges Way

Sometimes, as part of a cooking demonstration, I take the group on a field trip to the nearest supermarket. There's no better place to share my discoveries about which healthy products taste best, which are best for you, and which healthy products don't deliver enough taste to include in my recipes.

While I'd certainly enjoy accompanying you to your neighborhood store, we'll have to settle for a field trip *on paper*. I've tasted and tried just about every fat- and sugar-free product on the market, but so many new ones keep coming all the time, you're going to have to learn to play detective on your own. I've turned label reading into an art, but often the label doesn't tell me everything I need to know.

Sometimes you'll find, as I have, that the product with *no* fat doesn't provide the taste satisfaction you require; other times, a no-fat or low-fat product just doesn't cook up the same way as the original product. And some foods, including even the leanest meats, can't eliminate *all* the fat. That's okay, though—a healthy diet should include anywhere from 15 to 25 percent of total calories from fat on any given day.

Take my word for it—your supermarket is filled with lots of delicious foods that can and should be part of your healthy diet for life. Come, join me as we check it out on the way to the checkout!

First stop, the **salad dressing** aisle. Salad dressing is usually a high-fat food, but there are great alternatives available. Let's look first at the regular Ranch dressing—2 tablespoons have 170 calories and 18 grams of fat—and who can eat just 2 tablespoons? Already, that's about half the fat grams most people should consume in a day. Of course, it's the most flavorful too. Now let's look at the low-fat version. Two tablespoons have 110 calories and 11 grams of fat; they took about half of the fat out, but there's still a lot of sugar there. The fat-free version has 50 calories and zero grams of fat, but they also took most of the flavor out. Here's what you do to get it back: add a tablespoon of fat-free mayonnaise, a few more parsley flakes, and about a half teaspoon of sugar substitute to your 2-tablespoon serving. That trick, with the fat-free mayo and sugar substitute, will work with just about any fat-free dressing and give it more of that full-bodied flavor of the high-fat version. Be careful not to add too much sugar substitute—you don't want it to become sickeningly sweet.

I use Kraft fat-free **mayonnaise** at 10 calories per tablespoon to make scalloped potatoes, too. The Smart Beat brand is also a good one.

Before I buy anything at the store, I read the label carefully: the total fat plus the saturated fat; I look to see how many calories are in a realistic serving, and I say to myself, Would I eat that much—or would I eat more? I look at the sodium and I look at the total carbohydrates. I like to check those ingredients because I'm cooking for diabetics and heart patients too. And I check the total calories from fat.

Remember that 1 fat gram equals 9 calories, while 1 protein or 1 carbohydrate gram equals 4 calories.

A wonderful new product is I Can't Believe It's Not Butter! spray, with zero calories and zero grams of fat in four squirts. It's great for your air-popped popcorn. As for **light margarine spread**, beware—most of the fat-free brands don't melt on toast, and they don't taste very good either, so I just leave them on the shelf. For the few times I do use a light margarine I tend to buy Smart Beat Ultra, Promise Ultra, or Weight Watchers Light Ultra. The number-one ingredient in them is water. I occasionally use the light margarine in cooking, but I don't really put margarine on my toast anymore. I use apple butter or make a spread with fat-free cream cheese mixed with a little spreadable fruit instead.

So far, Pillsbury hasn't released a reduced-fat **crescent roll**, so you'll only get one crescent roll per serving from me. I usually make eight of the rolls serve twelve by using them for a crust. The house brands may be lower in fat, but they're usually not as good flavor wise—and don't quite cover the pan when you use them to make a crust. If you're going to use crescent rolls with lots of other stuff on top, then a house brand might be fine.

The Pillsbury French Loaf makes a wonderful **pizza crust** and fills a giant jelly-roll pan. One-fifth of this package "costs" you only 1 gram of fat (and I don't even let you have that much!). Once you use this for your pizza crust, you will never go back to anything else instead. I use it to make calzones too.

I only use Philadelphia fat-free **cream cheese** because it has the best consistency. I've tried other brands, but I wasn't happy with them. Healthy Choice makes lots of great products, but their cream cheese just doesn't work as well with my recipes.

Let's move to the **cheese** aisle. My preferred brand is Kraft ⅓ Less Fat Shredded Cheeses. I will not use the fat-free versions because *they don't melt*. I would gladly give up sugar and fat, but I will not give up flavor. This is a happy compromise. I use the reduced-fat version, I use less, and I use it where your eyes "eat" it, on top of the recipe. So you walk away satisfied and with a finished product that's very low in fat. If you want to make grilled cheese sandwiches for your kids, use the Kraft ⅓ Less Fat cheese slices, and it'll taste exactly like the one they're used to. The fat-free will not.

Some brands have come out with a fat-free **hot dog**, but the ones we've tasted haven't been very good. So far, among the low-fat brands, I think Healthy Choice tastes the best. Did you know that regular hot dogs have as many as 15 grams of fat?

Dubuque's Extra-Lean Reduced-Sodium **ham** tastes wonderful, reduces the sodium as well as the fat, and gives you a larger serving. Don't be fooled by products called turkey ham; they may *not* be lower in fat than a very lean pork product. Here's one label as an example: I checked a brand of turkey ham called Genoa. It gives you a 2-ounce serving for 70 calories and 3½ grams of fat. The Dubuque extra-lean ham, made from pork, gives you a 3-ounce serving for 90 calories, but only 2½ grams of fat. *You get more food and less fat.*

The same can be true for packaged **ground turkey;** if you're not buying *fresh* ground turkey, you may be getting a product with turkey skin and a lot of fat ground up in it. Look to be sure the package is labeled with the fat content; if it isn't, run the other way!

Your best bets in **snack foods** are pretzels, which are always low in fat, as well as the chips from the Guiltless Gourmet, which taste especially good with one of my dips.

Frozen dinners can be expensive and high in sodium, but it's smart to have two or three in the freezer as a backup when your best-laid plans go awry and you need to grab something on the run. But it's not a good idea to rely on them too much—what if you can't get to the store to get them, or you're short on cash? The sodium can be high in some of them because they often replace the fat with salt, so do read the labels. Also ask yourself if the serving is enough to satisfy you; for many of us, it's not.

Egg substitute is expensive, and probably not necessary unless you're cooking for someone who has to worry about every bit of cholesterol in their diet. If you occasionally have a fried egg or an omelet, *use the real egg.* For cooking, you can usually substitute two egg whites for one whole egg. Most of the time it won't make any difference, but check your recipe carefully.

Frozen pizzas aren't particularly healthy, but used occasionally, in moderation, they're okay. Your best bet is to make your own using the Pillsbury French Crust. Take a look at the frozen pizza package of your choice, though, because you may find that plain cheese pizza, which you might think would be the healthiest, might actually have the most fat. Since there's nothing else on there, they have to cover the crust with a heavy layer of high-fat cheese. A veggie pizza generally uses less cheese and more healthy, crunchy vegetables.

Healthy frozen desserts are hard to find except for the Weight Watchers brands. I've always felt that their portions are so small, and for their size still pretty high in fat and sugar. (This is one of the reasons I think I'll be successful marketing my frozen desserts someday. After Cliff tasted one of my earliest healthy pies—and licked the plate clean—he remarked that if I ever opened a restaurant, people would keep coming back for my desserts alone!) Keep an eye out for fat-free or very low-fat frozen yogurt or sorbet products. Even Häagen-Dazs, which makes some of the highest fat content ice cream, now has a fat-free fruit sorbet pop out that's pretty good. I'm sure there will be more before too long.

You have to be realistic: what are you willing to do, and what are you *not* willing to do? Let's take bread, for example. Some people just have to have the real thing—rye bread with caraway seeds or a whole-wheat version with bits of bran in it.

I prefer to use reduced-calorie **bread** because I like a *real* sandwich. This way, I can have two slices of bread and it counts as only one bread/starch exchange.

Do you love **croutons?** Forget the ones from the grocery store—they're extremely high in fat. Instead, take reduced-calorie bread, toast it, give it a quick spray of I Can't Believe It's Not Butter! Spray, and let it dry a bit. Cut the bread in cubes. Then, for an extra-good flavor, put the pieces in a plastic bag with a couple of tablespoons of Kraft House Italian (a reduced-fat Parmesan/Romano cheese blend) and shake them up. You might be surprised just how good they are! Another product that's really good for a crouton—Corn Chex cereal. Sprinkle a few Chex on top of your salad, and I think you'll be pleasantly surprised. I've also found that Rice Chex, crushed up, with parsley flakes and a little bit of Parmesan cheese, makes a great topping for casseroles that you used to put potato chips on.

Salad toppers can make a lot of difference in how content you feel after you've eaten. Some low-fat cheese, some homemade croutons, and even some bacon bits on top of your greens deliver an abundance of tasty satisfaction. I always use the real Hormel **bacon bits** instead of the imitation bacon-flavored bits. I only use a small amount, but you get that real bacon flavor—and less fat too.

How I Shop for Myself

I always keep my kitchen stocked with my basic staples; that way, I can go to the cupboard and create new recipes any time I'm inspired. I hope you will take the time (and allot the money) to stock your cupboards with items from the staples list, so you can enjoy developing your own healthy versions of family favorites without making extra trips to the market.

I'm always on the lookout for new products sitting on the grocery shelf. When I spot something I haven't seen before, I'll usually grab it, glance at the front, then turn it around and read the label carefully. I call it looking at the promises (the "come-on" on the front of the package) and then at the warranty (the ingredients list and the label on the back).

If it looks as good on the back as it does on the front, I'll say okay and either create a recipe on the spot or take it home for when I do think of something to do with it. Picking up a new product is just about the only time I buy something not on my list.

The items on my shopping list are normal, everyday foods, but as low-fat and low-sugar (*while still tasting good*) as I can find. I can make any recipe in this book as long as these staples are on my shelves. After using these products for a couple of weeks, you will find it becomes routine to have them on hand. And I promise you, I really don't spend any more at the store now than I did a few years ago when I told myself I couldn't afford some of these items. Back then, of course, plenty of unhealthy, high-priced snacks I really didn't need somehow made the magic leap from the grocery shelves into my cart. Who was I kidding?

Yes, you often have to pay a little more for fat-free or low-fat products, including meats. But since I frequently use a half pound of meat to serve four to six people, your cost per serving will be much lower.

Try adding up what you were spending before on chips and cookies, premium brand ice cream and fatty cuts of meat, and you'll soon see that we've *streamlined* your shopping cart, and taken the weight off your pocketbook as well as your hips!

Remember, your good health is *your* business—but it's big business too. Write to the manufacturers of products you and your family enjoy but feel are just too high in fat, sugar, or sodium to be part of your new healthy lifestyle. Companies are spending millions of dollars to respond to consumers' concerns about food products, and I bet that in the next few years, you'll discover fat-free and low-fat versions of nearly every product piled high on your supermarket shelves!

The Healthy

Exchanges Kitchen

You might be surprised to discover I still don't have a massive test kitchen stocked with every modern appliance and handy gadget ever made. The tiny galley kitchen where I first launched Healthy Exchanges has room for only one person at a time, but it never stopped me from feeling the sky's the limit when it comes to seeking out great healthy taste!

Because storage is at such a premium in my kitchen, I don't waste space with equipment I don't really need. Here's a list of what I consider worth having. If you notice serious gaps in your equipment, you can probably find most of what you need at a local discount store or garage sale. If your kitchen is equipped with more sophisticated appliances, don't feel guilty about using them. Enjoy every appliance you can find room for or that you can afford. Just be assured that healthy, quick, and delicious food can be prepared with the "basics."

A Healthy Exchanges Kitchen Equipment List

Good-quality nonstick skillets (medium, large)
Good-quality saucepans (small, medium, large)
Glass mixing bowls (small, medium, large)
Glass measures (1-cup, 2-cup, 4-cup, 8-cup)
Sharp knives (paring, chef, butcher)
Rubber spatulas
Wire whisks
Measuring spoons
Measuring cups
Large mixing spoons
Egg separator
Covered jar
Vegetable parer

Grater
Potato masher
Electric mixer
Electric blender
Electric skillet
4-inch round custard dishes
Glass pie plates
8-by-8-inch glass baking dishes
Cake pans (9-by-9, 9-by-13-inch)
10¾-by-7-by-1½-inch biscuit pan
Cookie sheets (good nonstick ones)
Jelly-roll pan
Muffin tins
5-by-9-inch bread pan
Plastic colander
Cutting board
Pie wedge server
Cooking timer
Slow cooker
Air popper for popcorn
Kitchen scales (unless you *always* use my recipes)
Wire racks for cooling baked goods
Electric toaster oven (to conserve energy for those times when only one
    item is being baked or for a recipe that requires a short baking time)
Square-shaped server
Can opener (I prefer manual)
Rolling pin

How to Read a Healthy Exchanges Recipe

The Healthy Exchanges Nutritional Analysis

Before using these recipes you may wish to consult your physician or health-care provider to be sure they are appropriate for you. The information in this book is not intended to take the place of any medical advice. It reflects my experiences, studies, research, and opinions regarding healthy eating.

Each recipe includes nutritional information calculated in three ways:

Healthy Exchanges Weight Loss Choices™ or Exchanges
Calories, fiber, and fat grams
Diabetic exchanges

In every Healthy Exchanges recipe, the diabetic exchanges have been calculated by a Registered Dietitian. All the other calculations were done by computer, using the Food Processor II software. When the ingredient listing gives more than one choice, the first ingredient listed is the one used in the recipe analysis. Due to inevitable variations in the ingredients you choose to use, the nutritional values should be considered approximate.

The annotation "(limited)" following Protein counts in some recipes indicates that consumption of whole eggs should be limited to four per week.

Please note the following symbols:

☆This star means read the recipe's directions carefully for special instructions about **division** of ingredients.

❄This symbol indicates **FREEZES WELL**.

A Few Cooking Terms
to Ease the Way

Everyone can learn to cook *The Healthy Exchanges Way*. It's simple, it's quick, and the results are delicious! If you've tended to avoid the kitchen because you find recipe instructions confusing or complicated, I hope I can help you feel more confident. I'm not offering a full cooking course here, just some terms I use often that I know you'll want to understand.

Bake:	To cook food in the oven; sometimes called roasting
Beat:	To mix very fast with a spoon, wire whisk, or electric mixer
Blend:	To mix two or more ingredients together thoroughly so that the mixture is smooth
Boil:	To cook in liquid until bubbles form
Brown:	To cook at low to medium-low heat until ingredients turn brown
Chop:	To cut food into small pieces with a knife, blender, or food processor
Combine:	To mix ingredients together with a spoon
Cool:	To let stand at room temperature until food is no longer hot to the touch
Dice:	To chop into small, even-sized pieces
Drain:	To pour off liquid; sometimes you will need to reserve the liquid to use in the recipe, so please read carefully.
Drizzle:	To sprinkle drops of liquid (for example, chocolate syrup) lightly over top of food
Fold in:	To combine delicate ingredients with other foods by using a gentle, circular motion. Example: adding Cool Whip Lite to an already stirred-up bowl of pudding.
Preheat:	To heat your oven to the desired temperature, usually about 10 minutes before you put your food in to bake
Sauté:	To cook in skillet or frying pan until food is soft
Simmer:	To cook in a small amount of liquid over low heat; this lets the

flavors blend without too much liquid evaporating.

Whisk: To beat with a wire whisk until mixture is well mixed; don't worry about finesse here, just use some elbow grease!

How to Measure

I try to make it as easy as possible by providing more than one measurement for many ingredients in my recipes—both the weight in ounces and the amount measured by a measuring cup, for example. Just remember:

- You measure **solids** (flour, Cool Whip Lite, yogurt, macaroni, nonfat dry milk powder) in your set of separate measuring cups (¼, ⅓, ½, 1 cup)

- You measure **liquids** (Diet Mountain Dew, water, tomato juice) in the clear glass or plastic measuring cups that measure ounces, cups, and pints. Set the cup on a level surface and pour the liquid into it, or you may get too much.

- You can use your measuring spoon set for liquids or solids. **Note:** Don't pour a liquid like an extract into a measuring spoon held over the bowl in case you overpour; instead, do it over the sink.

Here are a few handy equivalents:

3 teaspoons	equals	1 tablespoon
4 tablespoons	equals	¼ cup
5⅓ tablespoons	equals	⅓ cup
8 tablespoons	equals	½ cup
10⅔ tablespoons	equals	⅔ cup
12 tablespoons	equals	¾ cup
16 tablespoons	equals	1 cup
2 cups	equals	1 pint
4 cups	equals	1 quart
8 ounces liquid	equals	1 fluid cup

That's it. Now, ready, set, cook!

The Recipes

Soups and Salads

These tasty recipes stir up so quickly, they almost make themselves! Even if the clock is ticking and you have no idea what to serve for dinner, pick any page in this section, and you're on your way fast! Grande Corn Chili is oh-so-fast and filling, you'll serve it often, and my Waldorf Chicken-Rice Salad couldn't be easier or quicker to mix and fix!

Italian Cream of Tomato Noodle Soup

Did you think that living healthy meant giving up "cream" soups forever? You know I don't believe in deprivation, so instead I found a way to work magic, turning good-for-you ingredients into a truly luscious treat!

◐ Serves 4 (1½ cups)

3 cups Healthy Request Tomato Juice or any reduced-sodium tomato juice
2 teaspoons Italian seasoning
2 teaspoons dried onion flakes
1¾ cups (3 ounces) uncooked noodles
1 (10¾-ounce) can Healthy Request Tomato Soup
1½ cups (one 12-fluid-ounce can) Carnation Evaporated Skim Milk
¼ teaspoon black pepper
¼ cup (¾ ounce) grated Kraft fat-free Parmesan cheese

In a large saucepan, combine tomato juice, Italian seasoning, onion flakes, and uncooked noodles. Cook over medium heat for 10 minutes or until noodles are tender. Add tomato soup, evaporated skim milk, and black pepper. Mix well to combine. Lower heat and simmer for 5 minutes, stirring often. When serving, top each bowl with 1 tablespoon Parmesan cheese.

Each serving equals:

HE: 1½ Vegetable • 1 Bread • ¾ Skim Milk • ¼ Protein •
½ Slider • 5 Optional Calories

274 Calories • 2 gm Fat • 14 gm Protein • 50 gm Carbohydrate •
562 mg Sodium • 307 mg Calcium • 3 gm Fiber

DIABETIC: 1½ Vegetable • 1½ Starch • ½ Skim Milk

Grande Corn Chili

I often say that my recipes are so easy, children can prepare them. Well, once your kids are old enough to use a can opener and the stove, they're ready to make this tangy, tasty dish!   ☻   Serves 4 (1½ cups)

> 1 (10¾-ounce) can Healthy Request Tomato Soup
> 1½ cups water
> 1 cup chunky salsa (mild, medium, or hot)
> 10 ounces (one 16-ounce can) red kidney beans, rinsed and drained
> 2 cups frozen whole-kernel corn, thawed
> 1½ teaspoons chili seasoning
> 1 teaspoon dried parsley flakes

In a medium saucepan, combine tomato soup, water, and salsa. Stir in kidney beans, corn, chili seasoning, and parsley flakes. Bring mixture to a boil. Lower heat and simmer for 10 minutes, stirring occasionally.

HINT: Thaw corn by placing in a colander and rinsing under hot water for one minute.

Each serving equals:

HE: 1¼ Protein • 1 Bread • ½ Vegetable • ½ Slider •
5 Optional Calories

193 Calories • 1 gm Fat • 7 gm Protein • 39 gm Carbohydrate •
346 mg Sodium • 68 mg Calcium • 7 gm Fiber

DIABETIC: 2 Starch • 1 Meat • 1 Vegetable

Tex-Mex Chicken Cheese Soup

Ever enjoyed chicken tacos at your favorite Mexican restaurant? *Mmm-mmm*, me too, so I decided to create a soup that sizzles with all those flavors. Serve it hot, or if your family prefers it, use really hot salsa, and serve it HOT-HOT-HOT!

● Serves 4 (1½ cups)

2 cups (one 16-ounce can) Healthy Request Chicken Broth
½ cup chunky salsa (mild, medium, or hot)
1 (10¾-ounce) can Healthy Request Cream of Chicken Soup
½ cup (one 2.5-ounce jar) sliced mushrooms, drained
1 cup (5 ounces) finely-diced cooked chicken breast
1½ cups frozen whole-kernel corn, thawed
⅓ cup Carnation Nonfat Dry Milk Powder
½ cup water
¼ teaspoon black pepper
¾ cup (3 ounces) shredded Kraft reduced-fat Cheddar cheese

In a large saucepan, combine chicken broth, salsa, chicken soup, mushrooms, chicken, and corn. Bring mixture to a boil. Meanwhile, in a small bowl, combine dry milk powder and water. Stir milk mixture into chicken mixture. Add black pepper and Cheddar cheese. Mix well to combine. Lower heat and simmer for 5 minutes or until cheese melts, stirring often.

HINTS: 1. If you don't have leftovers, purchase a chunk of   cooked chicken breast from your local deli.
2. Thaw corn by placing in a colander and rinsing under hot water for one minute.

Each serving equals:

HE: 2¼ Protein • ¾ Bread • ½ Vegetable • ¼ Skim Milk • ½ Slider • 13 Optional Calories

250 Calories • 6 gm Fat • 23 gm Protein • 26 gm Carbohydrate • 971 mg Sodium • 258 mg Calcium • 2 gm Fiber

DIABETIC: 1½ Meat

Beefy Mushroom Noodle Soup

Soup is a terrific way to use up leftovers without making your kids feel as if they're eating "Oh, that again?" This recipe has so much old-fashioned flavor, they might go looking for Grandma in the kitchen! ☻ Serves 4 (1½ cups)

1 full cup (6-ounces) diced cooked lean roast beef
½ cup chopped onion
1¾ cups (one 14½-ounce can) Swanson Beef Broth
2¼ cups water
⅛ teaspoon black pepper
1 teaspoon dried onion flakes
1¾ cups (3 ounces) uncooked noodles
1 cup (one 4-ounce jar) sliced mushrooms, drained
1 teaspoon dried parsley flakes

In a large saucepan sprayed with butter-flavored cooking spray, sauté roast beef and onion for 5 minutes. Add beef broth, water, black pepper, and onion flakes. Mix well to combine. Bring mixture to a boil. Stir in uncooked noodles, mushrooms, and parsley flakes. Lower heat and simmer for 15 minutes, or until noodles are tender, stirring occasionally.

HINT: If you don't have leftovers, purchase a chunk of cooked lean roast beef from your local deli.

Each serving equals:

HE: 1½ Protein • 1 Bread • ¾ Vegetable • 8 Optional Calories

162 Calories • 2 gm Fat • 13 gm Protein • 23 gm Carbohydrate • 821 mg Sodium • 17 mg Calcium • 2 gm Fiber

DIABETIC: 1½ Meat • 1 Starch

Magic Micro Chili

I love this dish for those steamy summer nights when the last thing you want to do is slave over a hot stove. You'll find that the microwave produces a lot less shrinkage than browning meat in a skillet does, and it also keeps all the tasty flavor in! ☻ Serves 4 (1½ cups)

8 ounces ground 90% lean turkey or beef
½ cup chopped onion
½ cup chopped green bell pepper
1¾ cups (one 15-ounce can) Hunt's Chunky Tomato Sauce
1¾ cups (one 14½-ounce can) Swanson Beef Broth
10 ounces (one 16-ounce can) red kidney beans, rinsed and drained
1½ teaspoons chili seasoning
¼ teaspoon black pepper
½ cup (1½ ounces) slightly crushed Doritos Reduced Fat Nacho Chips
4 tablespoons fat-free sour cream

Place meat, onion, and green pepper in a plastic colander and set colander in a 9-inch glass pie plate. Microwave on HIGH (100% power) for 3 to 4 minutes, or until meat is browned, stirring after 2 minutes. In an 8-cup glass measuring bowl, combine browned meat mixture, tomato sauce, and beef broth. Stir in kidney beans, chili seasoning, and black pepper. Cover and continue microwaving on Medium (50% power) for 15 minutes, turning bowl and stirring after 6 minutes. When serving, garnish each bowl with 2 tablespoons crushed nacho chips and 1 tablespoon sour cream.

Each serving equals:

HE: 2¾ Protein • 2½ Vegetable • ½ Bread • ¼ Slider •
3 Optional Calories

226 Calories • 6 gm Fat • 17 gm Protein • 26 gm Carbohydrate •
981 mg Sodium • 41 mg Calcium • 7 gm Fiber

DIABETIC: 2 Meat • 2 Vegetable • 1 Starch

Easy Pastafazool

Here's a spicy quick-and-hearty soup that "eats like a meal!" It's a great choice if you're trying to trim back your meat budget, too. ☻   Serves 6 (1½ cups)

8 ounces ground 90% lean turkey or beef

½ cup chopped onion

6 ounces (one 10-ounce can) red kidney beans, rinsed and drained

1¾ cups (one 15-ounce can) Hunt's Chunky Tomato Sauce

1¾ cups (one 14½-ounce can) Swanson Beef Broth

1¾ cups water

1⅓ cups (3 ounces) uncooked elbow macaroni

2 tablespoons chili seasoning

2 tablespoons Italian seasoning

¼ cup (¾ ounce) grated Kraft fat-free Parmesan cheese

In a large saucepan sprayed with olive oil–flavored cooking spray, brown meat and onion. Add kidney beans, tomato sauce, beef broth, water, uncooked macaroni, chili seasoning, and Italian seasoning. Mix well to combine. Bring mixture to a boil. Lower heat, cover, and simmer for 15 minutes or until macaroni is tender. Just before serving, stir in Parmesan cheese.

Each serving equals:

HE: 1⅔ Protein • 1⅓ Vegetable • ⅔ Bread • 6 Optional Calories

184 Calories • 4 gm Fat • 12 gm Protein • 25 gm Carbohydrate • 796 mg Sodium • 13 mg Calcium • 4 gm Fiber

DIABETIC: 1½ Meat • 1 Vegetable • 1 Starch/Carbohydrate

Tomato Patch Chicken Rice Soup

◐ Serves 4 (1½ cups)

1 full cup (6 ounces) diced cooked chicken breast
2 cups (one 16-ounce can) Healthy Request Chicken Broth
2 cups water
1¾ cups (one 15-ounce can) Hunt's Chunky Tomato Sauce
1 cup (3 ounces) uncooked instant rice
1 teaspoon dried parsley flakes
¼ teaspoon black pepper

In a large saucepan, combine chicken breast, chicken broth, water, and tomato sauce. Bring mixture to a boil. Lower heat and simmer for 5 minutes. Stir in rice, parsley flakes, and black pepper. Remove from heat, cover, and let set for 5 minutes. Stir again just before serving.

HINT: If you don't have leftovers, purchase a chunk of cooked chicken breast from your local deli.

Each serving equals:

HE: 1¾ Vegetable • 1½ Protein • ¾ Bread • 16 Optional Calories

105 Calories • 1 gm Fat • 16 gm Protein • 8 gm Carbohydrate • 340 mg Sodium • 0 gm Fiber

DIABETIC: 1½ Meat • 1 Vegetable • ½ Starch

Neapolitan Corn Chowder

● Serves 4 (1½ cups)

2 cups (10 ounces) diced raw potatoes
2 cups (one 16-ounce can) Healthy Request Chicken Broth
1 cup frozen whole kernel corn
1¾ cups (one 15-ounce can) Hunt's Chunky Tomato Sauce
½ cup (one 2.5-ounce jar) sliced mushrooms, drained
1 teaspoon Italian seasoning
2 teaspoons Sugar Twin or Sprinkle Sweet
½ teaspoon dried minced garlic
2 teaspoons dried parsley flakes

In a medium saucepan, combine potatoes and chicken broth. Cook over medium heat for 10 minutes or until potatoes are tender. Add corn, tomato sauce, mushrooms, Italian seasoning, Sugar Twin, garlic, and parsley flakes. Bring mixture to a boil. Lower heat and simmer for about 10 minutes, stirring occasionally.

Each serving equals:

HE: 2 Vegetable • 1 Bread • 9 Optional Calories

132 Calories • 0 gm Fat • 6 gm Protein • 27 gm Carbohydrate • 832 mg Sodium • 1 gm Fiber

DIABETIC: 2 Vegetable • 1 Starch

Roman Holiday Tomato Rice Soup

● Serves 4 (1½ cups)

½ cup finely chopped onion

½ finely chopped green bell pepper

4 cups (two 16-ounce cans) tomatoes, coarsely chopped and undrained

1 cup water

2 teaspoons Italian seasoning

⅛ teaspoon black pepper

¼ cup (1 ounce) sliced ripe olives

⅓ cup (2 ounces) chopped Canadian bacon or any extra-lean ham

⅔ cup (2 ounces) uncooked instant rice

In a large saucepan sprayed with olive oil-flavored cooking spray, sauté onion and green pepper for 5 minutes or until tender. Meanwhile, place undrained tomatoes in a blender container. Cover and process on BLEND for 30 seconds. Add pureed tomatoes and water into saucepan with onion and green pepper. Mix well to combine. Stir in Italian seasoning, black pepper, olives, and Canadian bacon. Bring mixture to a boil. Stir in rice. Remove from heat, cover, and let set for 5 minutes. Stir again just before serving.

Each serving equals:

HE: 2½ Vegetable • ½ Protein • ½ Bread • ¼ Fat

110 Calories • 2 gm Fat • 5 gm Protein • 18 gm Carbohydrate • 291 mg Sodium • 3 gm Fiber

DIABETIC: 2 Vegetable • ½ Meat • ½ Starch

Jiffy Tomato Soup

○ Serves 4 (1 cup)

1¾ cups (one 15-ounce can) Hunt's Chunky Tomato Sauce
1 (10¾-ounce) can Healthy Request Tomato Soup
½ teaspoon baking soda
2 teaspoons Sugar Twin or Sprinkle Sweet
1½ cups (one 12-fluid-ounce can) Carnation Evaporated Skim Milk
½ teaspoon black pepper
1 teaspoon chili seasoning mix

In a medium saucepan, combine tomato sauce and tomato soup. Cook over medium heat until mixture starts to boil, stirring often. Stir in baking soda, Sugar Twin, evaporated skim milk, black pepper, and chili seasoning mix. Lower heat and simmer for 5 minutes or until mixture is heated through, stirring constantly.

Each serving equals:

HE: 1¾ Vegetable • ¾ Skim Milk • ½ Slider • 6 Optional Calories

157 Calories • 1 gm Fat • 9 gm Protein • 28 gm Carbohydrate •
957 mg Sodium • 3 gm Fiber

DIABETIC: 2 Vegetable • 1 Skim Milk

Ham and Cabbage-Bean Soup

This intensely flavorful soup is rich and satisfying—not to mention jam-packed with nourishing, low-fat ingredients that fill you up, not out!

○ Serves 4 (1½ cups)

½ cup diced onion

2 cups water

1 full cup (6 ounces) diced Dubuque 97% fat-free ham or any extra-lean ham

2 cups shredded cabbage

2 cups (one 16-ounce can) tomatoes, coarsely chopped, and undrained

1 teaspoon chili seasoning

¼ teaspoon black pepper

10 ounces (one 16-ounce can) great northern beans, rinsed and drained

In a large saucepan sprayed with butter-flavored cooking spray, sauté onion for 5 minutes or until tender. Add water, ham, cabbage, undrained tomatoes, chili seasoning, and black pepper. Mix well to combine. Bring mixture to a boil. Stir in great northern beans. Lower heat, cover, and simmer for 15 minutes.

Each serving equals:

HE: 2¼ Vegetable • 2¼ Protein

170 Calories • 2 gm Fat • 14 gm Protein • 24 gm Carbohydrate • 376 mg Sodium • 74 mg Calcium • 6 gm Fiber

DIABETIC: 2 Meat • 1½ Vegetable • 1 Starch

Cucumber-Tomato-Lettuce Salad

When your garden is overflowing with ripe, fresh veggies like cukes and tomatoes, shred a lovely head of lettuce and top it off with this fresh and creamy combo of summer's best! ● Serves 4

½ cup Kraft fat-free mayonnaise
⅓ cup Land O Lakes no-fat sour cream
1 cup diced unpeeled cucumber
2 cups diced fresh tomatoes, drained
2 tablespoons finely chopped onion
1 teaspoon dried parsley flakes
6 cups shredded lettuce

In a medium bowl, combine mayonnaise and sour cream. Fold in cucumber, tomatoes, onion, and parsley flakes. For each serving, place 1½ cups lettuce on a plate and spoon about ¾ cup vegetable mixture over top.

Each serving equals:

HE: 4½ Vegetable • ½ Slider

72 Calories • 0 gm Fat • 2 gm Protein • 16 gm Carbohydrate • 303 mg Sodium • 46 mg Calcium • 2 gm Fiber

DIABETIC: 2½ Vegetable • ½ Starch/Carbohydrate

Crunchy Kidney Bean Salad

There's lots of good nourishment in a can of kidney beans, and this salad provides a pretty setting to serve them in. There's also a nice mix of textures—crunchy and creamy. ☻ Serves 4 (¾ cup)

> 10 ounces (one 16-ounce can) red kidney beans, rinsed and drained
> ¾ cup diced celery
> ½ cup diced green bell pepper
> ¼ cup finely chopped onion
> ½ cup Kraft fat-free mayonnaise
> 1 teaspoon dried parsley flakes
> ⅛ teaspoon black pepper

In a medium bowl, combine kidney beans, celery, green pepper, and onion. Add mayonnaise, parsley flakes, and black pepper. Mix well to combine. Cover and refrigerate for at least 15 minutes. Gently stir again just before serving.

Each serving equals:

HE: 1¼ Protein • ¾ Vegetable • ¼ Slider

64 Calories • 0 gm Fat • 3 gm Protein • 13 gm Carbohydrate •
267 mg Sodium • 18 mg Calcium • 3 gm Fiber

DIABETIC: ½ Meat • ½ Starch

Salsa Grande Tossed Salad

I bet you never thought about tossing your salad greens with your favorite salsa, but it makes for a fresh and delightful change! And yes, I do mean corn chips—the real kind—just enough to win over your taste buds!!   ☻   Serves 4

1 cup chunky salsa (mild, medium, or hot)
¼ cup Kraft Fat Free Ranch Dressing
¼ cup Kraft fat-free mayonnaise
6 cups shredded lettuce
1 cup (3 ounces) coarsely crushed Doritos Reduced Fat Nacho Chips

In a medium bowl, combine salsa, Ranch dressing, and mayonnaise. For each serving, place 1½ cups lettuce on a plate, spoon about ⅓ cup salsa mixture over lettuce, and top with ¼ cup crushed chips.

Each serving equals:

HE: 3½ Vegetable • 1 Bread • ¼ Slider • 5 Optional Calories

148 Calories • 4 gm Fat • 3 gm Protein • 25 gm Carbohydrate • 645 mg Sodium • 100 mg Calcium • 2 gm Fiber

DIABETIC: 2½ Vegetable • 1 Starch

Garden Noodle Salad

Whenever I make pasta or noodles, I like to boil up a few extra cups to keep in the fridge for last-minute cold salads like this tasty one. It's colorful and full of flavor, a wonderful accompaniment for any grilled meat or fish, so heat up the barbecue and go for it! ☻ Serves 6 (1 cup)

> 2 cups cold cooked noodles, rinsed and drained
> 1 cup chopped fresh mushrooms
> ½ cup diced green bell pepper
> ¼ cup chopped green onion
> 1 cup chopped fresh broccoli
> ½ cup shredded carrots
> ¾ cup cherry tomatoes
> ⅓ cup (1½ ounces) sliced ripe olives
> ½ cup Kraft Fat Free Italian Dressing
> ¼ cup Kraft fat-free mayonnaise

In a large bowl, combine noodles, mushrooms, green pepper, green onion, broccoli, carrots, tomatoes, and olives. In a small bowl, combine Italian dressing and mayonnaise. Pour dressing mixture over noodle mixture. Mix gently to combine. Cover and refrigerate for at least 20 minutes. Gently stir again just before serving.

HINT: 1¾ cups uncooked noodles usually cooks to about 2 cups.

Each serving equals:

HE: 1⅓ Vegetable • 1 Bread • ¼ Fat • ¼ Slider •
8 Optional Calories

113 Calories • 1 gm Fat • 4 gm Protein • 22 mg Carbohydrate •
371 mg Sodium • 26 mg Calcium • 2 gm Fiber

DIABETIC: 1½ Vegetable • 1 Starch • ½ Fat

Rice Zucchini Salad

Zucchini is one of those garden vegetables that appears in such abundance each summer, the smart cook is always on the lookout for new ways to serve it. This one combines a variety of tastes and textures in a tangy dressing, and it's sure to make your zucchini harvest more of a celebration than ever!

☻ Serves 4 (1 cup)

2 cups cold cooked rice
½ cup diced green bell pepper
½ cup chopped fresh mushrooms
1 cup diced unpeeled zucchini
¼ cup Kraft Fat Free Italian Dressing
2 tablespoons Kraft fat-free mayonnaise

In a medium bowl, combine rice, green pepper, mushrooms, and zucchini. Add Italian Dressing and mayonnaise. Mix well to combine. Cover and refrigerate for at least 15 minutes. Gently stir again just before serving.

HINT: 1⅓ cups uncooked rice usually cooks to about 2 cups.

Each serving equals:

HE: 1 Bread • 1 Vegetable • 13 Optional Calories

100 Calories • 0 gm Fat • 2 gm Protein • 23 gm Carbohydrate • 242 mg Sodium • 15 mg Calcium • 2 gm Fiber

DIABETIC: 1 Starch/Carbohydrate • ½ Vegetable

Waldorf Chicken-Rice Salad

When you invite your closest friends over for a card party, this dish makes a lovely presentation. Why not serve lunch on the patio, where these elegant and healthy ingredients—the pale green grapes, the soft green of fresh celery—offer a delightful picture-on-a-plate! ☻ Serves 6 (¾ cup)

> *1 cup (2 small) unpeeled, cored and diced Red Delicious apples*
> *1 tablespoon lemon juice*
> *1 cup cold cooked rice*
> *1 cup (5 ounces) diced cooked chicken breast*
> *1 cup diced celery*
> *1 cup (6 ounces) seedless green grapes*
> *¼ cup (1 ounce) chopped walnuts*
> *½ cup Kraft fat-free mayonnaise*

In a large bowl, combine apples and lemon juice. Add rice, chicken, celery, grapes, walnuts, and mayonnaise. Mix gently to combine. Cover and refrigerate for at least 15 minutes. Gently stir again just before serving.

HINTS: 1. ⅔ cup uncooked rice usually cooks to about 1 cup.
  2. If you don't have leftovers, purchase a chunk of cooked chicken breast from your local deli.

Each serving equals:

HE: 1 Protein • ⅔ Fruit • ⅓ Bread • ⅓ Vegetable • ⅓ Fat • 13 Optional Calories

148 Calories • 4 gm Fat • 9 gm Protein • 19 gm Carbohydrate • 299 mg Sodium • 23 mg Calcium • 1 gm Fiber

DIABETIC: 1 Fruit • 1 Meat

Banana-Apple Waldorf Salad

I've added a few new "wrinkles" to the classic Waldorf salad by tumbling some tasty banana bits and a few marshmallows into this creamy apple concoction. So much good-for-you flavor in a dish that couldn't be prettier! (Remember, leave the skin on the apples for that extra fiber!)　❤　Serves 4 (½ cup)

> 1 cup (1 medium) diced banana
> 1 cup (2 small) unpeeled, cored and diced Red Delicious apples
> ¼ cup (1 ounce) chopped walnuts
> ½ cup finely chopped celery
> ½ cup (1 ounce) miniature marshmallows
> ½ cup Cool Whip Free
> 1 tablespoon Kraft fat-free mayonnaise

In a medium bowl, combine banana, apples, walnuts, celery, and marshmallows. Add Cool Whip Free and mayonnaise. Mix well to combine. Cover and refrigerate for at least 15 minutes. Gently stir again just before serving.

HINT:　To prevent banana from turning brown, mix with 1 teaspoon lemon juice or sprinkle with Fruit Fresh.

Each serving equals:

HE: 1 Fruit • ½ Fat • ¼ Protein • ¼ Vegetable • ¼ Slider • 10 Optional Calories

141 Calories • 5 gm Fat • 1 gm Protein • 23 gm Carbohydrate • 19 mg Sodium • 11 mg Calcium • 2 gm Fiber

DIABETIC: 1 Fruit • ½ Fat • ½ Starch/Carbohydrate

Mandarin Orange Spinach Salad

⟳ Serves 6 (1⅓ cups)

1 cup (one 11-ounce can) mandarin oranges, rinsed and drained

2 cups chopped fresh cauliflower

¼ cup chopped green bell pepper

2¾ cups fresh torn spinach leaves, stems discarded

¼ cup Kraft Fat Free Ranch Dressing

½ cup unsweetened orange juice

2 tablespoons Kraft fat-free mayonnaise

In a large bowl, combine mandarin oranges, cauliflower, green pepper, and spinach leaves. In a small bowl, combine Ranch dressing, orange juice, and mayonnaise. Add dressing mixture to spinach mixture. Toss gently to combine. Serve at once.

Each serving equals:

HE: 1⅔ Vegetable • ½ Fruit • ¼ Slider

60 Calories • 0 gm Fat • 2 gm Protein • 13 gm Carbohydrate • 171 mg Sodium • 2 gm Fiber

DIABETIC: 1 Vegetable • ½ Fruit

Royal Carrot and Celery Salad

⏺ Serves 4 (¾ cup)

1½ cups shredded carrots

1 cup finely chopped celery

2 tablespoons (½ ounce) chopped walnuts

⅓ cup Kraft fat-free mayonnaise

1 teaspoon lemon juice

Sugar substitute to equal 2 teaspoons sugar

Lettuce leaves

In a medium bowl, combine carrots, celery, and walnuts. In a small bowl, combine mayonnaise, lemon juice, and sugar substitute. Add mayonnaise mixture to carrot mixture. Mix well to combine. Cover and refrigerate for at least 20 minutes. Gently stir again just before serving. Serve on lettuce leaves.

Each serving equals:

HE: 1¼ Vegetable • ¼ Fat • ¼ Slider

58 Calories • 2 gm Fat • 1 gm Protein • 9 gm Carbohydrate • 182 mg Sodium • 2 gm Fiber

DIABETIC: 2 Vegetable

Mediterranean Vegetable Salad

⚫ Serves 4 (full ¾ cup)

2 cups chopped fresh tomatoes

1 cup unpeeled chopped cucumbers

⅓ cup (1½ ounces) shredded Kraft reduced-fat mozzarella cheese

1 tablespoon chopped fresh parsley or 1 teaspoon dried parsley flakes

¼ cup Kraft Fat Free Italian Dressing

In a large bowl, combine tomatoes, cucumbers, mozzarella cheese, and parsley. Add Italian dressing. Mix gently to combine. Cover and refrigerate for at least 20 minutes. Gently stir again just before serving.

Each serving equals:

HE: 1½ Vegetable • ½ Protein • 4 Optional Calories

58 Calories • 2 gm Fat • 4 gm Protein • 6 gm Carbohydrate • 259 mg Sodium • 1 gm Fiber

DIABETIC: 1 Vegetable • ½ Fat

Italian Radish and Pea Salad

● Serves 4 (⅔ cup)

2 cups frozen peas, thawed
½ cup finely chopped radishes
½ cup Kraft Fat Free Italian Dressing

In a medium bowl, combine peas and radishes. Add Italian dressing. Mix gently to combine. Cover and refrigerate for at least 20 minutes. Gently stir again just before serving.

HINT: Thaw peas by placing in a colander and rinsing under hot water for one minute.

Each serving equals:

HE: 1 Bread • ¼ Vegetable • 8 Optional Calories

68 Calories • 0 gm Fat • 4 gm Protein • 13 gm Carbohydrate • 287 mg Sodium • 4 gm Fiber

DIABETIC: 1 Starch

Garden Patch Salad

● Serves 4 (1 cup)

½ cup unpeeled diced zucchini
1 cup diced fresh tomatoes
½ cup diced green bell pepper
½ cup diced onion
½ cup chopped radishes
½ cup thinly sliced carrots
½ cup thinly sliced celery
¼ cup Kraft Fat Free French Dressing
2 tablespoons Kraft Fat Free Italian Dressing
1 tablespoon fresh parsley or 1 teaspoon dried parsley flakes

In a large bowl, combine zucchini, tomatoes, green pepper, onion, radishes, carrots, and celery. In a small bowl, combine French dressing, Italian dressing, and parsley. Pour dressing mixture over vegetables. Mix gently to combine. Cover and refrigerate for at least 20 minutes. Gently stir again just before serving.

Each serving equals:

HE: 2 vegetable • ¼ Slider • 7 Optional Calories

52 Calories • 0 gm Fat • 1 gm Protein • 12 gm Carbohydrate • 217 mg Sodium • 2 gm Fiber

DIABETIC: 2 Vegetable

Provence Cucumber Salad

○ Serves 4 (½ cup)

¼ cup Kraft Fat Free French Dressing
1 tablespoon Kraft fat-free mayonnaise
1 tablespoon Dijon mustard
2 tablespoons chopped fresh parsley or 1 teaspoon dried parsley flakes
2¼ cups unpeeled thinly sliced cucumbers
¼ cup finely chopped onion

In a medium bowl, combine French dressing, mayonnaise, mustard, and parsley. Add cucumbers and onion. Mix gently to combine. Cover and refrigerate for at least 20 minutes. Gently stir again just before serving.

Each serving equals:

HE: 1¼ Vegetable • ¼ Slider • 13 Optional Calories

28 Calories • 0 gm Fat • 0 gm Protein • 7 gm Carbohydrate • 149 mg Sodium • 1 gm Fiber

DIABETIC: 1 Vegetable

Italian Tomato Mozzarella Salad

🕐 Serves 4 (full ⅔ cup)

2 cups cherry tomatoes, quartered

3 tablespoons (¾ ounce) shredded Kraft reduced-fat mozzarella cheese

¼ cup Kraft Fat Free Ranch Dressing

2 tablespoons Kraft Fat Free Ranch Dressing

2 tablespoons Kraft Fat Free Italian Dressing

1 tablespoon fresh parsley or 1 teaspoon dried parsley flakes

In a medium bowl, combine tomatoes and mozzarella cheese. In a small bowl, combine Ranch dressing and Italian dressing. Pour dressing mixture over tomato mixture. Add parsley. Mix gently to combine. Cover and refrigerate for at least 15 minutes. Gently stir again just before serving.

Each serving equals:

HE: 1 Vegetable • ¼ Protein • ¼ Slider • 7 Optional Calories

57 Calories • 1 gm Fat • 2 gm Protein • 10 gm Carbohydrate • 289 mg Sodium • 1 gm Fiber

DIABETIC: 2 Vegetable

Mexican Bean Salad

◐ Serves 6 (⅔ cup)

4 cups (two 16-ounce cans) cut green beans, rinsed and drained
¼ cup finely chopped onion
¼ cup finely chopped green bell pepper
1½ cups frozen whole kernel corn, thawed
½ cup Kraft Fat Free French Dressing
1 teaspoon chili seasoning mix
¾ cup (3 ounces) shredded Kraft reduced-fat Cheddar cheese

In a large bowl, combine green beans, onion, green pepper, and corn. Add French dressing. Mix well to combine. Stir in chili seasoning mix and Cheddar cheese. Cover and refrigerate for at least 20 minutes. Gently stir again just before serving.

HINT: Thaw corn by placing in a colander and rinsing under hot water for one minute.

Each serving equals:

HE: 1½ Vegetable • ⅔ Protein • ½ Bread • 17 Optional Calories

117 Calories • 1 gm Fat • 7 gm Protein • 20 gm Carbohydrate •
359 mg Sodium • 3 gm Fiber

DIABETIC: 1 Vegetable • 1 Starch

Calico Cucumber Salad

● Serves 4 (1 cup)

2 cups frozen whole kernel corn, thawed
2¾ cups unpeeled thinly sliced cucumbers
¼ cup finely chopped onion
½ cup Kraft fat-free mayonnaise
2 tablespoons white vinegar
Sugar substitute to equal 1 tablespoon sugar
¼ teaspoon black pepper
1 teaspoon dried parsley flakes

In a large bowl, combine corn, cucumber, and onion. In a small bowl, combine mayonnaise, vinegar, sugar substitute, black pepper, and parsley flakes. Add mayonnaise mixture to vegetable mixture. Stir gently to combine. Cover and refrigerate for at least 20 minutes. Gently stir again just before serving.

HINT: Thaw corn by placing in a colander and rinsing under hot water for one minute.

Each serving equals:

HE: 1½ Vegetable • 1 Bread • ¼ Slider • 2 Optional Calories

108 Calories • 0 gm Fat • 3 gm Protein • 24 gm Carbohydrate •
217 mg Sodium • 3 gm Fiber

DIABETIC: 1 Vegetable • 1 Starch

Italian Green Bean Salad

● Serves 8 (¾ cup)

½ cup Kraft Fat Free Italian Dressing

2 tablespoons Kraft fat-free mayonnaise

½ cup (1½ ounces) grated Kraft fat-free Parmesan cheese

6 cups (three 16-ounce cans) cut green beans, rinsed and drained

1½ cups chopped fresh tomatoes

½ cup finely chopped onion

½ cup (2 ounces) sliced ripe olives

In a large bowl, combine Italian dressing, mayonnaise, and Parmesan cheese. Stir in green beans. Add tomatoes, onion, and olives. Mix well to combine. Cover and refrigerate for at least 20 minutes. Gently stir again just before serving.

Each serving equals:

HE: 2 Vegetable • ¼ Protein • ¼ Fat • 7 Optional Calories

77 Calories • 1 gm Fat • 4 gm Protein • 13 gm Carbohydrate • 319 mg Sodium • 4 gm Fiber

DIABETIC: 2½ Vegetable

Cauliflower Pea Salad

● Serves 6 (full ¾ cup)

2 cups chopped fresh cauliflower
1½ cups frozen peas, thawed
¾ cup chopped celery
¼ cup chopped onion
½ cup Kraft fat-free mayonnaise
¼ cup Kraft Fat Free Ranch Dressing
1 teaspoon dried parsley flakes
Sugar substitute to equal 2 teaspoons sugar

In a large bowl, combine cauliflower, peas, celery, and onion. In a small bowl, combine mayonnaise, Ranch dressing, parsley flakes, and sugar substitute. Add dressing mixture to vegetable mixture. Mix gently to combine. Cover and refrigerate for at least 20 minutes. Gently stir again just before serving.

HINT: Thaw peas by placing in a colander and rinsing under hot water for one minute.

Each serving equals:

HE: 1 Vegetable • ½ Bread • ¼ Slider • 10 Optional Calories

72 Calories • 0 gm Fat • 3 gm Protein • 15 gm Carbohydrate • 269 mg Sodium • 3 gm Fiber

DIABETIC: 1 Vegetable • ½ Starch

Layered Honey Dijon Tomato Salad

○ Serves 6

1½ cups shredded lettuce

3 cups chopped fresh tomatoes

¾ cup (3 ounces) shredded Kraft reduced-fat mozzarella cheese

2 teaspoons dried parsley flakes

6 tablespoons Kraft Fat Free Honey Dijon Dressing

For each serving, layer ¼ cup lettuce on salad plate, place ½ cup tomatoes over lettuce, sprinkle about 2 tablespoons mozzarella cheese and ½ teaspoon parsley flakes over tomatoes and drizzle 1 tablespoon dressing over top. Serve at once.

Each serving equals:

HE: 1½ Vegetable • ⅔ Protein • ¼ Slider • 5 Optional Calories

74 Calories • 2 gm Fat • 4 gm Protein • 10 gm Carbohydrate • 240 mg Sodium • 1 gm Fiber

DIABETIC: 2 Vegetable • ½ Meat

Viva la Carrot Salad

❂ Serves 4 (full ½ cup)

2 cups shredded carrots
½ cup diced onion
¼ cup Kraft Fat Free French Dressing
1 teaspoon dried parsley flakes
2 tablespoons Kraft fat-free mayonnaise

In a medium bowl, combine carrots and onion. Add French dressing, parsley flakes, and mayonnaise. Mix gently to combine. Cover and refrigerate for at least 20 minutes. Gently stir again just before serving.

Each serving equals:

HE: 1¼ Vegetable • ¼ Slider • 2 Optional Calories

52 Calories • 0 gm Fat • 1 gm Protein • 12 gm Carbohydrate • 193 mg Sodium • 2 gm Fiber

DIABETIC: 2 Vegetable

Golden Broccoli Salad

❂ Serves 4 (1 cup)

3 cups chopped fresh broccoli

¾ cup shredded carrots

¼ cup chopped onion

⅓ cup (1½ ounces) shredded Kraft reduced-fat Cheddar cheese

2 tablespoons Hormel Bacon Bits

⅔ cup Kraft fat-free mayonnaise

Sugar substitute to equal 2 tablespoons sugar

1½ teaspoons prepared mustard

2 tablespoons skim milk

In a large bowl, combine broccoli, carrots, onion, Cheddar cheese, and bacon bits. In a small bowl, combine mayonnaise, sugar substitute, mustard, and skim milk. Add mayonnaise mixture to broccoli mixture. Mix gently to combine. Cover and refrigerate for at least 20 minutes. Gently stir again just before serving.

Each serving equals:

HE: 2 Vegetable • ½ Protein • ½ Slider • 5 Optional Calories

115 Calories • 3 gm Fat • 7 gm Protein • 15 gm Carbohydrate • 482 mg Sodium • 3 gm Fiber

DIABETIC: 2 Vegetable • ½ Meat

Dilly Veggie Salad

○ Serves 4 (1 cup)

1½ cups thinly sliced carrots
1¼ cups unpeeled chopped cucumbers
¾ cup thinly sliced radishes
1 cup chopped fresh broccoli
½ cup Kraft Fat Free Ranch Dressing
¼ cup Kraft fat-free mayonnaise
½ teaspoon dried dill weed

In a medium bowl, combine carrots, cucumbers, radishes, and broccoli. In a small bowl, combine Ranch dressing, mayonnaise, and dill weed. Add dressing mixture to vegetable mixture. Mix gently to combine. Cover and refrigerate for at least 20 minutes. Gently stir again just before serving.

Each serving equals:

HE: 2¼ Vegetable • ¾ Slider • 15 Optional Calories

88 Calories • 0 gm Fat • 1 gm Protein • 21 gm Carbohydrate • 389 mg Sodium • 2 gm Fiber

DIABETIC: 2 Vegetable • ½ Starch

Riviera Salad

● Serves 4 (1 cup)

2 cups unpeeled thinly sliced cucumbers
1½ cups chopped fresh tomato
½ cup finely chopped celery
½ cup Kraft Fat Free French Dressing
1 tablespoon fresh parsley or 1 teaspoon dried parsley flakes

In a medium bowl, combine cucumbers, tomato, and celery. Add French dressing and parsley. Mix gently to combine. Cover and refrigerate for at least 20 minutes. Gently stir again just before serving.

Each serving equals:

HE: 2 Vegetables • ½ Slider

56 Calories • 0 gm Fat • 1 gm Protein • 13 gm Carbohydrate • 261 mg Sodium • 1 gm Fiber

DIABETIC: 2 Vegetable

Cabbage Angel Salad

● Serves 6 (full ½ cup)

3 cups shredded cabbage

½ cup (1 ounce) miniature marshmallows

1 cup (1 medium) diced banana

1 cup (one 8-ounce can) crushed pineapple, packed in fruit juice, undrained

⅓ cup Kraft fat-free mayonnaise

In a medium bowl, combine cabbage, marshmallows, and banana. In a small bowl, combine undrained pineapple and mayonnaise. Add pineapple mixture to cabbage mixture. Mix well to combine. Cover and refrigerate for at least 20 minutes. Gently stir again just before serving.

HINT: To prevent banana from turning brown, mix with 1 teaspoon lemon juice or sprinkle with Fruit Fresh.

Each serving equals:

HE: 1 Vegetable • ⅔ Fruit • 17 Optional Calories

80 Calories • 0 gm Fat • 1 gm Protein • 19 gm Carbohydrate • 101 mg Sodium • 1 gm Fiber

DIABETIC: 1 Fruit • 1 Free Vegetable

Tropical Waldorf Salad

○ Serves 6 (½ cup)

1 cup (1 medium) diced banana

¼ cup raisins

1 cup (2 small) cored, unpeeled, and diced Red Delicious apples

1 cup diced celery

½ cup (1 ounce) miniature marshmallows

2 tablespoons (½ ounce) chopped pecans

½ cup Kraft fat-free mayonnaise

1 teaspoon lemon juice

2 teaspoons Brown Sugar Twin

½ teaspoon coconut extract

2 tablespoons flaked coconut

In a medium bowl, combine banana, raisins, apples, celery, marshmallows, and pecans. In a small bowl, combine mayonnaise, lemon juice, Brown Sugar Twin, and coconut extract. Add mayonnaise mixture to banana mixture. Mix gently to combine. Cover and refrigerate for at least 20 minutes. Gently stir again just before serving. When serving, sprinkle 1 teaspoon coconut over top of each.

HINTS: 1. To prevent banana from turning brown, mix with 1 teaspoon lemon juice or sprinkle with Fruit Fresh.
2. To plump up raisins without "cooking," place in a glass measuring cup and microwave on HIGH for 20 seconds.

Each serving equals:

HE: 1 Fruit • ⅓ Vegetable • ⅓ Fat • ¼ Slider • 7 Optional Calories

110 Calories • 2 gm Fat • 1 gm Protein • 22 gm Carbohydrate • 166 mg Sodium • 2 gm Fiber

DIABETIC: 1½ Fruit • ½ Fat

Chunky Carrot Salad

● Serves 8 (⅔ cup)

> 4 cups shredded carrots
> 1 cup (one 8-ounce can) pineapple chunks, packed in fruit juice, drained, and 2
>   tablespoons liquid reserved
> ½ cup raisins
> 1 cup chopped celery
> ⅔ cup Kraft fat-free mayonnaise
> Sugar substitute to equal 1 tablespoon sugar

In a large bowl, combine carrots, pineapple, raisins, and celery. In a small bowl, combine mayonnaise, sugar substitute, and reserved pineapple liquid. Add mayonnaise mixture to carrot mixture. Mix well to combine. Cover and refrigerate for at least 20 minutes. Gently stir again just before serving.

HINT: To plump up raisins without "cooking," place in glass measuring cup and microwave on HIGH for 20 seconds.

Each serving equals:

HE: 1¼ Vegetable • ¾ Fruit • 14 Optional Calories

88 Calories • 0 gm Fat • 1 gm Protein • 21 gm Carbohydrate • 166 mg Sodium • 2 gm Fiber

DIABETIC: 1 Vegetable • 1 Fruit

California Ranch Corn Salad

⏻ Serves 4 (¾ cup)

2 cups frozen whole kernel corn, thawed
1 cup diced fresh tomato
½ cup diced green bell pepper
¼ cup diced onion
¼ cup finely chopped fresh parsley
3 tablespoons Kraft Fat Free Ranch Dressing
1 tablespoon Kraft fat-free mayonnaise
Sugar substitute to equal 1 teaspoon sugar
¼ teaspoon black pepper

In a medium bowl, combine corn, tomato, green pepper, onion, and parsley. In a small bowl, combine Ranch dressing, mayonnaise, sugar substitute, and black pepper. Add dressing mixture to corn mixture. Mix well to combine. Cover and refrigerate for at least 20 minutes. Gently stir again just before serving.

HINT: Thaw corn by placing in a colander and rinsing with hot water for one minute.

Each serving equals:

HE: 1 Bread • 1 Vegetable • ¼ Slider • 2 Optional Calories

112 Calories • 0 gm Fat • 3 gm Protein • 25 gm Carbohydrate • 154 mg Sodium • 3 gm Fiber

DIABETIC: 1 Starch • 1 Vegetable

Carrot-Pea Salad

☻ Serves 4 (full ½ cup)

¼ cup Kraft Fat Free Ranch Dressing

2 tablespoons Kraft fat-free mayonnaise

2 teaspoons dried onion flakes

1 teaspoon dried parsley flakes

1 teaspoon lemon juice

Sugar substitute to equal 2 teaspoons sugar

2 cups (one 16-ounce can) sliced carrots, rinsed and drained

1½ cups frozen peas, thawed

In a medium bowl, combine Ranch dressing, mayonnaise, onion flakes, parsley flakes, lemon juice, and sugar substitute. Add carrots and peas. Mix well to combine. Cover and refrigerate for at least 20 minutes. Gently stir again just before serving.

HINT: Thaw peas by placing in a colander and rinsing under hot water for one minute.

Each serving equals:

HE: 1 Vegetable • ¾ Bread • ¼ Slider • 11 Optional Calories

96 Calories • 0 gm Fat • 4 gm Protein • 20 gm Carbohydrate • 260 mg Sodium • 6 gm Fiber

DIABETIC: 1 Vegetable • 1 Starch

Old-Time Spinach Salad

⟳ Serves 4 (1⅓ cups)

4 cups fresh torn spinach leaves, stems discarded
1 hard-boiled egg, chopped
2 tablespoons Hormel Bacon Bits
1 cup sliced fresh mushrooms
½ cup Kraft Fat Free French Dressing
1 tablespoon finely chopped onion
½ teaspoon Worcestershire sauce
1 tablespoon Brown Sugar Twin

In a medium bowl, combine spinach, egg, bacon bits, and mushrooms. In a small bowl, combine French dressing, onion, Worcestershire sauce, and Brown Sugar Twin. Add dressing mixture to spinach mixture. Toss well to coat. Serve at once.

HINT: If you want the look and feel of eggs without the cholesterol, toss out the yolk and dice the white.

Each serving equals:

HE: 2½ Vegetable • ¼ Protein (limited) • ¼ Slider •
19 Optional Calories

90 Calories • 2 gm Fat • 5 gm Protein • 13 gm Carbohydrate •
375 mg Sodium • 2 gm Fiber

DIABETIC: 2 Vegetable • ½ Fat

Festive Pea Salad

🌑 Serves 4 (¾ cup)

2 cups frozen peas, thawed
¼ cup chopped green onion
½ cup chopped celery
¾ cup chopped fresh cauliflower
¼ cup (1 ounce) chopped cashews
½ cup Kraft fat-free mayonnaise
1 teaspoon prepared mustard
Sugar substitute to equal 2 teaspoons sugar
1 hard-boiled egg, chopped

In a large bowl, combine peas, green onion, celery, cauliflower, and cashews. In a small bowl, combine mayonnaise, mustard, and sugar substitute. Add mayonnaise mixture to vegetable mixture. Mix well to combine. Fold in egg. Cover and refrigerate for at least 20 minutes. Gently stir again just before serving.

HINTS: 1. Thaw peas by placing in a colander and rinsing with hot water for one minute.
2. If you want the look and feel of eggs without the cholesterol, toss out the yolk and dice the white.

Each serving equals:

HE: 1 Bread • ¾ Vegetable • ½ Fat • ½ Protein (¼ limited) • ¼ Slider • 1 Optional Calorie

149 Calories • 5 gm Fat • 7 gm Protein • 19 gm Carbohydrate • 239 mg Sodium • 5 gm Fiber

DIABETIC: 1 Starch • 1 Vegetable • 1 Fat

Tomato and Cucumber Macaroni Salad

● Serves 4 (1 cup)

2 cups cold cooked macaroni, rinsed and drained

1 cup chopped fresh tomatoes

1 cup unpeeled chopped cucumbers

¾ cup (3 ounces) shredded Kraft reduced-fat Cheddar cheese

½ cup Kraft Fat Free Catalina Dressing

¼ cup fat-free mayonnaise

2 teaspoons Dijon mustard

1 teaspoon dried onion flakes

1 tablespoon fresh parsley or 1 teaspoon dried parsley flakes

In a medium bowl, combine macaroni, tomatoes, cucumbers, and Cheddar cheese. In a small bowl, combine Catalina dressing, mayonnaise, Dijon mustard, onion flakes, and parsley. Add dressing mixture to pasta mixture. Mix gently to combine. Cover and refrigerate for at least 20 minutes. Gently stir again just before serving.

HINT: 1⅓ cups uncooked macaroni usually cooks to about 2 cups.

Each serving equals:

HE: 1 Bread • 1 Vegetable • 1 Protein • ¼ Slider •
15 Optional Calories

220 Calories • 4 gm Fat • 10 gm Protein • 36 gm Carbohydrate •
641 mg Sodium • 2 gm Fiber

DIABETIC: 2 Starch • 1 Vegetable • 1 Meat

Old-Fashioned Apple Salad

☻ Serves 4 (¾ cup)

2 cups (4 small) cored, unpeeled, and diced Red Delicious apples
¼ cup raisins
¼ cup (1 ounce) chopped walnuts
½ cup Cool Whip Lite
2 tablespoons Kraft fat-free mayonnaise
1 teaspoon lemon juice
½ teaspoon apple pie spice

In a medium bowl, combine apples, raisins, and walnuts. In a small bowl, combine Cool Whip Lite, mayonnaise, lemon juice, and apple pie spice. Add Cool Whip Lite mixture to apple mixture. Mix gently to combine. Cover and refrigerate for at least 20 minutes. Gently stir again just before serving.

HINT: To plump up raisins without "cooking," place in a glass measuring cup and microwave on HIGH 20 seconds.

Each serving equals:

HE: 1½ Fruit • ½ Fat • ¼ Protein • ¼ Slider • 5 Optional Calories

129 Calories • 5 gm Fat • 1 gm Protein • 20 gm Carbohydrate • 55 mg Sodium • 2 gm Fiber

DIABETIC: 1½ Fruit • 1 Fat

Green Beans and Pimiento Salad

☯ Serves 4 (full ½ cup)

2 cups (one 16-ounce can) cut green beans, rinsed and drained
¼ cup finely chopped onion
¼ cup canned sliced pimientos
2 tablespoons Land O Lakes no-fat sour cream
¼ cup Kraft fat-free mayonnaise
1 tablespoon skim milk
Sugar substitute to equal 2 teaspoons sugar
¼ teaspoon black pepper

In a medium bowl, combine green beans, onion, and pimientos. In a small bowl, combine sour cream, mayonnaise, skim milk, sugar substitute, and black pepper. Add sour cream mixture to green bean mixture. Mix gently to combine. Cover and refrigerate for at least 20 minutes. Gently stir again just before serving.

Each serving equals:

HE: 1¼ Vegetable • ¼ Slider

40 Calories • 0 gm Fat • 2 gm Protein • 8 gm Carbohydrate • 121 mg Sodium • 1 gm Fiber

DIABETIC: 1 Vegetable

Thai Vegetable Pasta Salad

○ Serves 4 (¾ cup)

2 cups cold cooked rotini pasta, rinsed and drained

1½ cups fresh pea pods

¼ cup chopped red or green bell pepper

¼ cup sliced green onion

¼ cup (1 ounce) chopped dry-roasted peanuts

3 tablespoons Kraft fat-free mayonnaise

2 tablespoons reduced-sodium soy sauce

2 tablespoons lemon juice

Sugar substitute to equal 1 tablespoon sugar

2 tablespoons Peter Pan reduced-fat peanut butter

In a large bowl, combine rotini pasta, pea pods, red or green pepper, onion, and peanuts. In a medium bowl, combine mayonnaise, soy sauce, lemon juice, sugar substitute, and peanut butter. Mix well until smooth, using a wire whisk. Add mayonnaise mixture to pasta mixture. Mix gently to combine. Cover and refrigerate for at least 20 minutes. Gently stir again just before serving.

HINT: 1½ cups uncooked rotini pasta usually cooks to about 2 cups.

Each serving equals:

HE: 1 Bread • 1 Vegetable • 1 Fat • ¾ Protein • 9 Optional Calories

231 Calories • 7 gm Fat • 9 gm Protein • 33 gm Carbohydrate • 139 mg Sodium • 3 gm Fiber

DIABETIC: 1½ Starch • 1 Vegetable • 1 Fat • ½ Meat

Easy Potato Salad

● Serves 6 (¾ cup)

3 full cups (16 ounces) peeled and diced cooked potatoes
¾ cup finely chopped celery
¼ cup finely chopped onion
⅓ cup Kraft fat-free mayonnaise
2 teaspoons prepared mustard
1 tablespoon vinegar
Sugar substitute to equal 1 tablespoon sugar
2 tablespoons sweet pickle relish
¼ teaspoon black pepper

In a large bowl, combine potatoes, celery, and onion. In a small bowl, combine mayonnaise, mustard, vinegar, sugar substitute, pickle relish, and black pepper. Add mayonnaise mixture to potato mixture. Mix gently to combine. Cover and refrigerate for at least 20 minutes. Gently stir again just before serving.

Each serving equals:

HE: ⅔ Bread • ⅓ Vegetable • 19 Optional Calories

80 Calories • 0 gm Fat • 2 gm Protein • 18 gm Carbohydrate • 170 mg Sodium • 0 gm Fiber

DIABETIC: 1 Starch

Salsa Pasta Salad

● Serves 4 (full ½ cup)

⅓ cup Kraft fat-free mayonnaise
½ cup chunky salsa (mild, medium, or hot)
¼ teaspoon dried minced garlic
1 teaspoon dried parsley flakes
1½ cups cold cooked rotini pasta, rinsed and drained
½ cup frozen whole kernel corn, thawed

In a medium bowl, combine mayonnaise, salsa, garlic, and parsley flakes. Add rotini pasta and corn. Mix gently to combine. Cover and refrigerate for at least 20 minutes. Gently stir again just before serving.

HINTS: 1. 1 cup uncooked rotini pasta usually cooks to about 1½ cups.
2. Thaw corn by placing in a colander and rinsing under hot water for one minute.

Each serving equals:

HE: 1 Bread • ¼ Vegetable • 13 Optional Calories

104 Calories • 0 gm Fat • 3 gm Protein • 23 gm Carbohydrate • 251 mg Sodium • 1 gm Fiber

DIABETIC: 1½ Starch

Garden Patch Pea Salad

● Serves 6 (⅔ cup)

2 cups frozen peas, thawed
1 cup chopped fresh tomato
¾ cup chopped celery
¼ cup finely chopped onion
¼ cup Kraft Fat Free Thousand Island Dressing
¼ cup Kraft fat-free mayonnaise
1 tablespoon fresh parsley or 1 teaspoon dried parsley flakes

In a medium bowl, combine peas, tomato, celery, and onion. In a small bowl, combine Thousand Island dressing, mayonnaise, and parsley. Add dressing mixture to vegetable mixture. Mix gently to combine. Cover and refrigerate for at least 20 minutes. Gently stir again just before serving.

HINT: Thaw peas by placing in a colander and rinsing under hot water for one minute.

Each serving equals:

HE: ⅔ Bread • ⅔ Vegetable • 15 Optional Calories

68 Calories • 0 gm Fat • 3 gm Protein • 14 gm Carbohydrate • 175 mg Sodium • 3 gm Fiber

DIABETIC: 1 Vegetable • ½ Starch

Pineapple and Orange Cottage Salad

O Serves 8 (¾ cup)

1 cup (one 11-ounce can) mandarin oranges, rinsed and drained

2 cups (two 8-ounce cans) crushed pineapple, packed in fruit juice, drained

2 cups fat-free cottage cheese

1 (4-serving) package JELL-O sugar-free orange gelatin

1 cup Cool Whip Lite

In a medium bowl, combine mandarin oranges, crushed pineapple, and cottage cheese. Add dry gelatin. Mix well to combine. Blend in Cool Whip Lite. Cover and refrigerate for at least 20 minutes. Gently stir again just before serving.

Each serving equals:

HE: ¾ Fruit • ½ Protein • ¼ Slider • 5 Optional Calories

113 Calories • 1 gm Fat • 9 gm Protein • 17 gm Carbohydrate • 240 mg Sodium • 0 gm Fiber

DIABETIC: 1 Fruit • 1 Meat

Old-Time Green Bean Salad

○ Serves 4 (¾ cup)

4 cups (two 16-ounce cans) cut green beans, rinsed and drained
1 hard-boiled egg, chopped
1 tablespoon Hormel Bacon Bits
¼ cup dill pickle relish
1 teaspoon dried parsley flakes
1 teaspoon prepared mustard
¼ teaspoon black pepper
¼ cup Kraft fat-free mayonnaise

In a medium bowl, combine green beans, egg, and bacon bits. In a small bowl, combine dill pickle relish, parsley flakes, mustard, black pepper, and mayonnaise. Add dressing mixture to green bean mixture. Mix gently to combine. Cover and refrigerate for at least 20 minutes. Gently stir again just before serving.

HINT: If you want the look and feel of eggs without the cholesterol, toss out the yolk and dice the whites.

Each serving equals:

HE: 2 Vegetable • ¼ Protein (limited) • 16 Optional Calories

90 Calories • 2 gm Fat • 4 gm Protein • 14 gm Carbohydrate • 285 mg Sodium • 3 gm Fiber

DIABETIC: 2 Vegetable • ½ Fat

Calico Bean Salad

◐ Serves 6 (full ¾ cup)

10 ounces (one 16-ounce can) red kidney beans, rinsed and drained

1 cup frozen whole kernel corn, thawed

2 cups (one 16-ounce can) cut green beans, rinsed and drained

1 cup finely chopped celery

¼ cup Kraft Fat Free Italian Dressing

2 tablespoons Kraft fat-free mayonnaise

¼ cup (¾ ounce) grated Kraft fat-free Parmesan cheese

1 teaspoon dried parsley flakes

¼ teaspoon black pepper

In a large bowl, combine kidney beans, corn, green beans, and celery. In a small bowl, combine Italian dressing, mayonnaise, Parmesan cheese, parsley flakes, and black pepper. Add dressing mixture to vegetable mixture. Mix gently to combine. Cover and refrigerate for at least 15 minutes. Gently stir again just before serving.

HINT: Thaw corn by placing in a colander and rinsing under hot water for one minute.

Each serving equals:

HE: 1 Protein • 1 Vegetable • ⅓ Bread • 6 Optional Calories

92 Calories • 0 gm Fat • 5 gm Protein • 18 gm Carbohydrate • 103 mg Sodium • 6 gm Fiber

DIABETIC: 1 Vegetable • ½ Meat • ½ Starch

Vegetables and
Side Dishes

These scrumptious sides take only minutes to stir up while the main course bubbles away, but they'll make it seem as if you fussed for hours cooking over a hot stove! If you've got ten minutes, you can serve up culinary fireworks with my Fabulous Dijon Green Beans or delight your kids and husband with a wonderful platter of Onion-Bacon Fettuccine! The clock is ticking, and dinner's almost ready— already!

Orange-Glazed Carrots

You'll be delighted and amazed at how easily your microwave turns a few sliced carrots and some spreadable fruit into a luscious dish that's gorgeous enough to serve at a dinner party! Since carrots are already naturally sweet, this is a great way to highlight that sweetness—and provide a colorful addition to any feast.

○ Serves 4 (full ¾ cup)

4 cups (two 16-ounce cans) sliced carrots, rinsed and drained

2 teaspoons reduced-calorie margarine

1 teaspoon dried parsley flakes

2 tablespoons orange marmalade spreadable fruit

In an 8-cup glass measuring bowl, combine carrots, margarine, parsley flakes, and spreadable fruit. Cover and microwave on HIGH (100% power) for 5 minutes. Let set 2 to 3 minutes. Gently stir again just before serving.

Each serving equals:

HE: 2 Vegetable • ½ Fruit • ¼ Fat

65 Calories • 1 gm Fat • 1 gm Protein • 13 gm Carbohydrate • 71 mg Sodium • 37 mg Calcium • 2 gm Fiber

DIABETIC: 2 Vegetable • ½ Fruit

Tex-Mex Green Beans and Corn

This one's for my husband, Cliff, who could eat green beans at every meal—and who really loves Mexican food! Of course, he likes food so spicy there's smoke coming from his ears, but I ask him to add extra "heat" at the table since I like it mild. ☻ Serves 4 (1 cup)

1 (10¾-ounce) can Healthy Request Tomato Soup

½ cup chunky salsa (mild, medium, or hot)

2 tablespoons Hormel Bacon Bits

1 teaspoon chili seasoning

4 cups (two 16-ounce cans) cut green beans, rinsed and drained

1 cup frozen whole-kernel corn, thawed

In a large skillet, combine tomato soup, salsa, bacon bits, and chili seasoning. Bring mixture to a boil. Stir in green beans and corn. Lower heat and simmer for 5 minutes, or until mixture is heated through, stirring often.

HINT: Thaw corn by placing in a colander and rinsing under hot water for one minute.

Each serving equals:

HE: 2¼ Vegetable • ½ Bread • ½ Slider • 18 Optional Calories

133 Calories • 1 gm Fat • 5 gm Protein • 26 gm Carbohydrate • 380 mg Sodium • 45 mg Calcium • 3 gm Fiber

DIABETIC: 1 Vegetable • 1 Starch/Carbohydrate

Fabulous Dijon Green Beans

The French town of Dijon is famous all over the world for its tangy mustard, which gives even this simple veggie dish some international sparkle! One taste, and your family is sure to smile and say, "Ooh-la-la!"

☻ Serves 4 (¾ cup)

1½ cups (one 12-fluid-ounce can) Carnation Evaporated Skim Milk
3 tablespoons all-purpose flour
⅛ teaspoon black pepper
4 cups (two 16-ounce cans) whole green beans, rinsed and drained
1 tablespoon Dijon mustard
1 teaspoon dried parsley flakes

In a covered jar, combine evaporated skim milk, flour, and black pepper. Shake well to blend. Pour milk mixture into a medium saucepan sprayed with butter-flavored cooking spray. Cook over medium heat until mixture thickens, stirring constantly. Stir in green beans, mustard, and parsley flakes. Lower heat and simmer for 5 minutes, or until mixture is heated through, stirring occasionally.

Each serving equals:

HE: 2 Vegetable • ¾ Skim Milk • ¼ Bread

128 Calories • 0 gm Fat • 10 gm Protein • 22 gm Carbohydrate • 173 mg Sodium • 314 mg Calcium • 2 gm Fiber

DIABETIC: 1 Vegetable • 1 Skim Milk

French Green Beans

Cooking with fat-free dressings is one of my favorite "speedy secrets" when it comes to healthy recipes! When you add just a little cheese to the mix, you get a super-fast side dish that really tastes special.   ☻   Serves 4 (½ cup)

> 4 cups (two 16-ounce cans) French style green beans, rinsed and drained
> 2 teaspoons dried onion flakes
> ¼ cup Kraft Fat Free French Dressing
> 3 tablespoons (¾ ounce) shredded Kraft reduced-fat Cheddar cheese
> ¼ cup (one 2-ounce jar) chopped pimiento, undrained

In a large skillet sprayed with butter-flavored cooking spray, combine green beans, onion flakes, and French dressing. Add Cheddar cheese and undrained pimiento. Mix well to combine. Cover and simmer for 5 minutes, stirring occasionally. Serve at once.

Each serving equals:

HE: 2 Vegetable • ¼ Protein • ¼ Slider • 5 Optional Calories

61 Calories • 1 gm Fat • 2 gm Protein • 11 gm Carbohydrate • 200 mg Sodium • 60 mg Calcium • 1 gm Fiber

DIABETIC: 1½ Vegetable • ½ Starch/Carbohydrate

Sautéed Tomatoes with Basil

My mother always grew tomatoes in her garden, and ever since childhood I've enjoyed dicing beautifully ripe tomatoes and tossing them with any kind of pasta. Even if you don't have room or time to "grow your own," pick up some rosy-red ones at the nearest farmers' market and enjoy the bounty of a summer harvest!

☻ Serves 4 (1 cup)

4 cups peeled and coarsely chopped fresh tomatoes

½ cup chopped onion

1½ teaspoons dried basil

2 tablespoons Sugar Twin or Sprinkle Sweet

⅛ teaspoon black pepper

In a large skillet sprayed with olive oil–flavored cooking spray, combine tomatoes and onion. Stir in basil, Sugar Twin, and black pepper. Bring mixture to a boil. Lower heat and simmer for 15 minutes, or until vegetables are tender, stirring occasionally.

Each serving equals:

HE: 2¼ Vegetable • 3 Optional Calories

48 Calories • 0 gm Fat • 2 gm Protein • 10 gm Carbohydrate • 17 mg Sodium • 13 mg Calcium • 2 gm Fiber

DIABETIC: 2 Vegetable

Creamy Vegetable Side Dish

Peas, carrots, corn, beans—the veggies that husbands and kids tend to put on their "best-loved" list—but you can make what's good even better by blending them with this luscious stove-top sauce!   ☻   Serves 4 (¾ cup)

>   1 cup (one 8-ounce can) whole-kernel corn, rinsed and drained
>   1 cup (one 8-ounce can) peas, rinsed and drained
>   1 cup (one 8-ounce can) sliced carrots, rinsed and drained
>   1 cup (one 8-ounce can) cut green beans, rinsed and drained
>   2 teaspoons dried onion flakes
>   1 teaspoon dried parsley flakes
>   ¼ cup Land O Lakes no-fat sour cream

In a medium saucepan, combine corn, peas, carrots, and green beans. Add onion flakes and parsley flakes. Mix well to combine. Stir in sour cream. Simmer for 10 minutes, or until mixture is heated through, stirring occasionally. Serve at once.

Each serving equals:

HE: 1 Bread • 1 Vegetable • 15 Optional Calories

96 Calories • 0 gm Fat • 4 gm Protein • 20 gm Carbohydrate • 173 mg Sodium • 45 mg Calcium • 4 gm Fiber

DIABETIC: 1 Starch • 1 Vegetable

Peas in Pimiento-Cheese Sauce

This is a real old-fashioned cozy dish like my grandma used to serve at the boardinghouse. I think the peas and pimientos are so pretty on the plate, you won't be able to decide whether this scrumptious blend tastes or looks better!

○ Serves 4 (½ cup)

⅔ cup Carnation Nonfat Dry Milk Powder

¾ cup water

2 tablespoons all-purpose flour

⅛ teaspoon black pepper

⅓ cup (1½ ounces) shredded Kraft reduced-fat Cheddar cheese

1 teaspoon dried parsley flakes

1 teaspoon dried onion flakes

2 cups frozen peas, thawed

¼ cup (one 2-ounce jar) chopped pimiento, drained

In a covered jar, combine dry milk powder, water, flour, and black pepper. Shake well to blend. Pour milk mixture into a medium saucepan sprayed with butter-flavored cooking spray. Add Cheddar cheese, parsley flakes, and onion flakes. Mix well to combine. Cook over medium heat until sauce thickens and cheese melts, stirring often. Stir in peas and pimiento. Lower heat and simmer for 5 minutes, or until mixture is heated through, stirring occasionally.

Each serving equals:

HE: 1 Bread • ½ Skim Milk • ½ Protein • 15 Optional Calories

154 Calories • 2 gm Fat • 12 gm Protein • 22 mg Carbohydrate • 298 mg Sodium • 272 mg Calcium • 4 gm Fiber

DIABETIC: 1 Starch • ½ Skim Milk • ½ Meat

Corn and Tomato Sauté

At our house, corn is served often, and not just because we live in the middle of the Iowa cornfields! It's a starchy vegetable so portion control is necessary, but you'll find that a reasonable serving of this tasty skillet combo fills your tummy with happiness. ☻ Serves 4 (¾ cup)

½ cup chopped onion

1¾ cups (one 15-ounce can) Hunt's Chunky Tomato Sauce

2 cups frozen whole-kernel corn, thawed

1 teaspoon chili seasoning

2 teaspoons Sugar Twin or Sprinkle Sweet

In a large skillet sprayed with butter-flavored cooking spray, sauté onion for 5 minutes or just until tender. Add tomato sauce, corn, chili seasoning, and Sugar Twin. Mix well to combine. Lower heat, cover, and simmer for 10 minutes, stirring occasionally.

HINT: Thaw corn by placing in a colander and rinsing under hot water for one minute.

Each serving equals:

HE: 2 Vegetable • 1 Bread • 1 Optional Calorie

108 Calories • 0 gm Fat • 3 gm Protein • 24 gm Carbohydrate • 705 mg Sodium • 6 mg Calcium • 4 gm Fiber

DIABETIC: 2 Vegetable • 1 Starch

Mexicali Corn

Here's an easy side dish that sparkles with fiesta colors and fiery flavors! If you really want to make it fun, mix red and green peppers for an even more festive touch.   ●   Serves 4 (½ cup)

½ cup chopped green bell pepper
½ cup chopped onion
2 cups frozen whole-kernel corn, thawed
1 teaspoon chili seasoning
1 teaspoon dried parsley flakes
¼ cup (one 2-ounce jar) chopped pimiento, undrained

In a large skillet sprayed with olive oil–flavored cooking spray, sauté green pepper and onion for 5 minutes or until tender. Add corn, chili seasoning, parsley flakes, and undrained pimiento. Mix well to combine. Lower heat, cover, and simmer for 10 minutes, stirring occasionally.

HINT: Thaw corn by placing in a colander and rinsing under hot water for one minute.

Each serving equals:

HE: 1 Bread • ½ Vegetable

92 Calories • 0 gm Fat • 3 gm Protein • 20 gm Carbohydrate • 273 mg Sodium • 11 mg Calcium • 3 gm Fiber

DIABETIC: 1 Starch

Ranch Hand Beans

Ring that dinner bell and call your hungry family together for this thrifty, filling feast! Even if you're not planning to round up stray cattle today, why not serve this quick-and-hearty recipe—and feel energized for hours?

☻ Serves 6 (¾ cup)

½ cup chopped onion
½ cup chopped green bell pepper
20 ounces (two 16-ounce cans) great northern beans, rinsed and drained
1¾ cups (one 15-ounce can) Hunt's Chunky Tomato Sauce
1 tablespoon Brown Sugar Twin
1 teaspoon chili seasoning
¼ teaspoon black pepper

In a large skillet sprayed with olive oil–flavored cooking spray, sauté onion and green pepper for 5 minutes or just until tender. Stir in great northern beans, tomato sauce, Brown Sugar Twin, chili seasoning, and black pepper. Lower heat and simmer for 10 minutes, or until mixture is heated through, stirring occasionally.

Each serving equals:

HE: 1⅔ Protein • 1⅓ Vegetable • 1 Optional Calorie

136 Calories • 0 gm Fat • 9 gm Protein • 25 gm Carbohydrate • 469 mg Sodium • 67 mg Calcium • 7 gm Fiber

DIABETIC: 1 Meat • 1 Vegetable • 1 Starch

Oriental Vegetables and Noodles

My sister Jeanie is what I call a "noncook cook," and this is the kind of Healthy Exchanges dish she loves. It just couldn't be easier, it couldn't be faster, and it couldn't taste any better than it already does! Stir it up tonight!

● Serves 4 (1 full cup)

> 3 cups purchased fresh or frozen stir-fry vegetables
> ½ cup water
> 1 (10¾-ounce) can Healthy Request Cream of Tomato Soup
> ⅓ cup skim milk
> 1 teaspoon dried parsley flakes
> ⅛ teaspoon black pepper
> 1 teaspoon reduced-sodium soy sauce
> 2 cups hot cooked noodles, rinsed and drained

In a large skillet, combine vegetables and water. Cover and cook over medium heat for 5 to 8 minutes or until vegetables are just tender. Add tomato soup, skim milk, parsley flakes, black pepper, and soy sauce. Mix well to combine. Stir in noodles. Lower heat and simmer for 5 minutes, stirring occasionally.

HINTS: 1. Any combination of your choice of raw vegetables may be used in place of purchased stir-fry vegetables.
2. 1¾ cups uncooked noodles usually cooks to about 2 cups.

Each serving equals:

HE: 1½ Vegetable • 1 Bread • ½ Slider • 4 Optional Calories

179 Calories • 3 gm Fat • 6 gm Protein • 32 gm Carbohydrate • 390 mg Sodium • 108 mg Calcium • 3 gm Fiber

DIABETIC: 1½ Vegetable • 1½ Starch/Carbohydrate

Rice and Corn Side Dish

I've always liked mixing veggies into the rice I serve my family—for one thing, it gives the dish lots of added color and flavor! This creamy, cheesy combo is a Lund favorite, the perfect "plate partner" for baked fish or grilled chicken.

❂ Serves 6 (1 cup)

1 cup finely chopped celery

½ cup chopped green bell pepper

½ cup chopped onion

1 cup hot cooked rice

2 cups frozen whole-kernel corn, thawed

⅔ cup Carnation Nonfat Dry Milk Powder

⅔ cup water

1½ cups (6 ounces) shredded Kraft reduced-fat Cheddar cheese

¼ cup (one 2-ounce jar) chopped pimiento, undrained

1 teaspoon dried parsley flakes

¼ teaspoon lemon pepper

In a large skillet sprayed with butter-flavored cooking spray, sauté celery, green pepper, and onion for 10 minutes or just until tender. Stir in rice and corn. In a small bowl, combine dry milk powder and water. Mix well to blend. Stir milk mixture into celery mixture. Add Cheddar cheese, undrained pimiento, parsley flakes, and lemon pepper. Mix well to combine. Lower heat, cover, and simmer for 5 minutes, stirring often.

HINTS: 1. ⅔ cup uncooked rice usually cooks to about 1 cup.
2. Thaw corn by placing in a colander and rinsing under hot water for one minute.

Each serving equals:

HE: 1⅓ Protein • 1 Bread • ⅔ Vegetable • ⅓ Skim Milk

---

193 Calories • 5 gm Fat • 13 gm Protein • 24 gm Carbohydrate • 331 mg Sodium • 315 mg Calcium • 2 gm Fiber

---

DIABETIC: 1½ Starch/Carbohydrate • 1 Meat

Roman Pasta

In the restaurant kitchen of a famous chef, this dish might be prepared with cream, but you can avoid the fat without sacrificing the flavor by stirring up this tasty combo that shimmers just like the Eternal City at night.

☺ Serves 4 (¾ cup)

>   1 cup (one 8-ounce can) Hunt's Tomato sauce
>   ⅓ cup Carnation Nonfat Dry Milk Powder
>   ½ cup (one 2.5-ounce jar) sliced mushrooms, drained
>   1 teaspoon Italian seasoning
>   ¼ teaspoon black pepper
>   1 teaspoon Sugar Twin or Sprinkle Sweet
>   2 cups hot cooked rotini pasta, rinsed and drained

In an 8-cup glass measuring bowl, combine tomato sauce, dry milk powder, mushrooms, Italian seasoning, black pepper, and Sugar Twin. Cover and microwave on HIGH (100% power) for 2 minutes. Mix well to combine. Stir in rotini pasta. Recover and microwave on HIGH for 2 minutes. Let set for 2 minutes before serving.

HINT: 1½ cups uncooked rotini pasta usually cooks to about 2 cups.

Each serving equals:

HE: 1¼ Vegetable • 1 Bread • ¼ Skim Milk • 1 Optional Calorie

132 Calories • 0 gm Fat • 6 gm Protein • 27 gm Carbohydrate • 515 mg Sodium • 77 mg Calcium • 2 gm Fiber

DIABETIC: 1½ Starch/Carbohydrate • 1 Vegetable

Stove-Top Vegetable Stuffing

If you've always cooked with just a sprinkle of salt and pepper, you may not know just how much wonderful flavor some lesser-known spices can add to a dish! Here's a fast-and-easy stuffing side dish that you can serve all year round, not just on the big "turkey holidays." ❤ Serves 8 (½ cup)

> *1 cup shredded carrots*
> *1 cup finely chopped celery*
> *1 cup finely chopped onion*
> *2 cups (one 16-ounce can) Healthy Request Chicken Broth*
> *4 cups (6 ounces) unseasoned whole-wheat and white dry bread cubes*
> *1 teaspoon dried crushed sage*
> *⅛ teaspoon black pepper*

In a large skillet sprayed with butter-flavored cooking spray, sauté carrots, celery, and onion for 10 minutes or just until tender. Add chicken broth. Mix well to combine. Stir in bread cubes, sage, and black pepper. Lower heat, cover, and simmer for 10 minutes, stirring occasionally.

HINT: Pepperidge Farm bread cubes work great.

Each serving equals:

HE: 1 Bread • ¾ Vegetable • 4 Optional Calories

113 Calories • 1 gm Fat • 4 gm Protein • 22 gm Carbohydrate • 380 mg Sodium • 6 mg Calcium • 2 gm Fiber

DIABETIC: 1 Starch • ½ Vegetable

Home-Style Green Beans

🌣 Serves 4 (1 cup)

4 cups (two 16-ounce cans) cut green beans, rinsed and drained
1 tablespoon dried onion flakes
2 tablespoons Hormel Bacon Bits
1 (10¾-ounce) can Healthy Request Cream of Mushroom Soup
¼ teaspoon black pepper
⅓ cup (1½ ounces) shredded Kraft reduced-fat Cheddar cheese

In a large skillet, combine green beans, onion flakes, and bacon bits. Cook over medium heat, stirring occasionally, for 5 minutes or until mixture is warmed through. Add mushroom soup, black pepper, and Cheddar cheese. Mix well to combine. Lower heat and simmer for 5 minutes or until cheese melts, stirring occasionally.

Each serving equals:

HE: 2 Vegetable • ½ Protein • ½ Slider • 14 Optional Calories

124 Calories • 4 gm Fat • 7 gm Protein • 15 gm Carbohydrate • 469 mg Sodium • 2 gm Fiber

DIABETIC: 2 Vegetable • ½ Meat • ½ Fat

Marinated Italian Green Beans

○ Serves 4 (½ cup)

2 cups (one 16-ounce can) Italian green beans, rinsed and drained
½ cup finely chopped onion
¼ cup Kraft Fat Free Italian Dressing

In a medium bowl, combine green beans and onion. Add Italian dressing. Toss gently to combine. Cover and refrigerate for at least 20 minutes. Gently stir again just before serving.

Each serving equals:

HE: 1¼ Vegetable • 4 Optional Calories

32 Calories • 0 gm Fat • 1 gm Protein • 7 gm Carbohydrate • 144 mg Sodium • 2 gm Fiber

DIABETIC: 1 Vegetable

Green Beans and Mushrooms

● Serves 4 (¾ cup)

½ cup chopped onion

1½ cups sliced fresh mushrooms

¼ cup (1 ounce) slivered almonds

1 (10¾-ounce) can Healthy Request Cream of Mushroom Soup

4 cups (two 16-ounce cans) cut green beans, rinsed and drained

¼ teaspoon black pepper

In a large skillet sprayed with butter-flavored cooking spray, sauté onion for 5 minutes or until tender. Add mushrooms and almonds. Mix well to combine. Continue cooking, stirring often, for 2 to 3 minutes. Stir in mushroom soup, green beans, and black pepper. Lower heat and simmer for 5 minutes or until mixture is heated through, stirring occasionally.

Each serving equals:

HE: 3 Vegetable • ½ Fat • ¼ Protein • ½ Slider • 1 Optional Calorie

125 Calories • 5 gm Fat • 4 gm Protein • 16 gm Carbohydrate • 323 mg Sodium • 4 gm Fiber

DIABETIC: 2 Vegetable • 1 Fat • ½ Starch

Continental Green Beans

● Serves 4 (full ¾ cup)

⅓ cup Kraft Fat Free Ranch Dressing
1 tablespoon dried minced onion
¼ teaspoon dried minced garlic
1 teaspoon Italian seasoning
4 cups (two 16-ounce cans) cut green beans, rinsed and drained

In a large saucepan, combine Ranch dressing, onion, garlic, and Italian seasoning. Mix well to combine. Stir in green beans. Cook over medium heat for 10 minutes or until mixture is heated through, stirring often.

Each serving equals:

HE: 2 Vegetable • ¼ Slider • 13 Optional Calories

64 Calories • 0 gm Fat • 2 gm Protein • 14 gm Carbohydrate • 165 mg Sodium • 4 gm Fiber

DIABETIC: 2 Vegetable

Rice and Peas Side Dish

○ Serves 4 (¾ cup)

½ cup (one 2.5-ounce jar) sliced mushrooms, drained

1 (10¾-ounce) can Healthy Request Cream of Mushroom Soup

1 cup skim milk

¼ teaspoon black pepper

½ cup frozen peas

1 cup (3 ounces) uncooked instant rice

1 teaspoon dried parsley flakes

In a large skillet, combine mushrooms, mushroom soup, skim milk, and black pepper. Stir in peas. Bring mixture to a boil. Stir in rice and parsley flakes. Remove from heat, cover, and let set for 5 minutes. Stir again just before serving.

Each serving equals:

HE: 1 Bread • ¼ Vegetable• ¼ Skim Milk • ½ Slider • 1 Optional Calorie

126 Calories • 2 gm Fat • 5 gm Protein • 22 gm Carbohydrate • 433 mg Sodium • 2 gm Fiber

DIABETIC: 1½ Starch

Adobe Vegetable Skillet

● Serves 6 (1 cup)

1½ cups coarsely chopped onion

1½ cups coarsely chopped green bell pepper

3 full cups (16 ounces) diced cooked potatoes

2 cups chopped fresh tomatoes

¼ cup taco sauce

½ teaspoon dried minced garlic

¼ teaspoon black pepper

In a large skillet sprayed with olive oil-flavored cooking spray, sauté onion and green pepper for 5 minutes. Add potatoes. Mix well to combine. Continue cooking for another 5 minutes, stirring often. Stir in tomatoes, taco sauce, garlic, and black pepper. Lower heat and simmer for 5 minutes or until mixture is heated through, stirring often.

HINT: I left skin on both potatoes and tomatoes, but you can peel them if you prefer.

Each serving equals:

HE: 1⅔ Vegetable • ⅔ Bread

110 Calories • 0 gm Fat • 3 gm Protein • 24 gm Carbohydrate • 93 mg Sodium • 3 gm Fiber

DIABETIC: 1 Vegetable • 1 Starch

"Real Man" Gazpacho

● Serves 4 (full 1 cup)

2 cups Healthy Request tomato juice or any reduced-sodium tomato juice
2½ cups chunky salsa (mild, medium, or hot)
1 teaspoon dried parsley flakes
¼ cup Land O Lakes no-fat sour cream

In a medium bowl, combine tomato juice, salsa, and parsley flakes. Refrigerate for at least 20 minutes. When serving, spoon mixture into mugs and top each with 1 tablespoon sour cream.

Each serving equals:

HE: 2¼ Vegetable • 15 Optional Calories

56 Calories • 0 gm Fat • 2 gm Protein • 12 gm Carbohydrate • 657 mg Sodium • 0 gm Fiber

DIABETIC: 2 Vegetable

Farmhouse Macaroni Bake

● Serves 6

1 cup hot cooked elbow macaroni, rinsed and drained

1 cup (one 8-ounce can) whole kernel corn, rinsed and drained

1 cup (one 8-ounce can) cream-style corn

¾ cup (3 ounces) shredded Kraft reduced-fat Cheddar cheese

1 teaspoon dried parsley flakes

¼ teaspoon black pepper

2 tablespoons Kraft Fat Free Catalina Dressing

Preheat oven to 350 degrees. Spray an 8-by-8-inch baking dish with butter-flavored cooking spray. In a medium bowl, combine macaroni, whole kernel corn, and cream-style corn. Stir in Cheddar cheese, parsley flakes, black pepper, and Catalina dressing. Pour mixture into prepared baking dish. Bake 25 minutes. Place baking dish on a wire rack and let set for 5 minutes. Divide into 6 servings.

HINT: ⅔ cup uncooked macaroni usually cooks to about 1 cup.

Each serving equals:

HE: 1 Bread • ⅔ Protein • 8 Optional Calories

---

134 Calories • 2 gm Fat • 7 gm Protein • 22 gm Carbohydrate • 283 mg Sodium • 1 gm Fiber

---

DIABETIC: 1½ Starch • ½ Meat

Creamy Green Beans and Onions

❂ Serves 6 (⅔ cup)

½ cup finely chopped onion

1½ cups (12-fluid-ounce can) Carnation Evaporated Skim Milk

3 tablespoons all-purpose flour

¼ teaspoon lemon pepper

4 cups (two 16-ounce cans) cut green beans, rinsed and drained

In a large skillet sprayed with butter-flavored cooking spray, sauté onion for 5 minutes or until tender. In a covered jar, combine evaporated skim milk and flour. Shake well to blend. Pour milk mixture into skillet with onion. Add lemon pepper. Mix well to combine. Continue cooking over medium heat for 5 minutes or until mixture thickens and starts to boil, stirring often. Stir in green beans. Lower heat and simmer for 5 minutes or until mixture is heated through, stirring occasionally.

Each serving equals:

HE: 1½ Vegetable • ½ Skim Milk • 15 Optional Calories

84 Calories • 0 gm Fat • 6 gm Protein • 15 gm Carbohydrate • 75 mg Sodium • 1 gm Fiber

DIABETIC: 1½ Vegetable • ½ Skim Milk

French Quarter Carrots

⚫ Serves 4 (full ⅔ cup)

4 cups shredded carrots
½ cup chopped onion
½ cup chopped green bell pepper
½ cup water
2 tablespoons Brown Sugar Twin
1 teaspoon prepared mustard
1 teaspoon dried parsley flakes
⅛ teaspoon black pepper

In a large skillet sprayed with butter-flavored cooking spray, sauté carrots, onion, and green pepper for 5 minutes, stirring often. Add water. Mix well to combine. Lower heat, cover and simmer for 10 minutes or until vegetables are tender and most of the liquid is evaporated, stirring occasionally. Stir in Brown Sugar Twin, mustard, parsley flakes, and black pepper. Continue cooking for 2 to 3 minutes, stirring often.

Each serving equals:

HE: 2½ Vegetable • 3 Optional Calories

56 Calories • 0 gm Fat • 1 gm Protein • 13 gm Carbohydrate • 46 mg Sodium • 2 gm Fiber

DIABETIC: 2 Vegetable

Blushing Cauliflower

● Serves 4 (¾ cup)

3 cups frozen cut cauliflower
1½ cups water
1 (10¾-ounce) can Healthy Request Tomato Soup
½ teaspoon dried minced garlic
2 teaspoons dried parsley flakes
1 teaspoon prepared mustard
¼ teaspoon lemon pepper
⅓ cup (1½ ounces) shredded Kraft reduced-fat Cheddar cheese

In a medium saucepan, cook cauliflower in water for 10 minutes or just until tender. Drain. In a large skillet, combine tomato soup, garlic, parsley flakes, mustard, and lemon pepper. Add Cheddar cheese. Mix well to combine. Stir in cauliflower. Lower heat and simmer for 5 minutes or until cheese melts, stirring often.

Each serving equals:

HE: 1½ Vegetable • ½ Protein • ½ Slider • 5 Optional Calories

111 Calories • 3 gm Fat • 5 gm Protein • 16 gm Carbohydrate • 453 mg Sodium • 5 gm Fiber

DIABETIC: 1½ Vegetable • ½ Starch

Grandma's "Baked" Beans

● Serves 6 (full ¾ cup)

1 cup finely chopped onion

½ cup finely chopped green bell pepper

2 tablespoons Hormel Bacon Bits

20 ounces (two 16-ounce cans) great northern beans, rinsed and drained

1¾ cups (one 15-ounce can) Hunt's Chunky Tomato Sauce

1 tablespoon Brown Sugar Twin

¼ teaspoon black pepper

In a large skillet sprayed with butter-flavored cooking spray, sauté onion, green pepper, and bacon bits for 5 minutes or until vegetables are tender. Add great northern beans, tomato sauce, Brown Sugar Twin, and black pepper. Mix well to combine. Lower heat and simmer for 20 minutes, stirring occasionally.

Each serving equals:

HE: 1⅔ Protein • 1⅔ Vegetable • 9 Optional Calories

141 Calories • 1 gm Fat • 9 gm Protein • 24 gm Carbohydrate • 101 mg Sodium • 6 gm Fiber

DIABETIC: 1 Starch • 1 Vegetable • 1 Meat

Schnitzel Carrots

● Serves 6 (1 cup)

½ cup finely chopped onion

1¾ cups (one 15-ounce can) Hunt's Chunky Tomato Sauce

¼ cup water

¼ teaspoon lemon pepper

2 tablespoons Brown Sugar Twin

1 tablespoon Sugar Twin or Sprinkle Sweet

1 teaspoon dried parsley flakes

4 cups (two 16-ounce cans) sliced carrots, rinsed and drained

2 tablespoons Hormel Bacon Bits

In a large skillet sprayed with butter-flavored cooking spray, sauté onion for 5 minutes or until tender. Add tomato sauce, water, lemon pepper, Brown Sugar Twin, Sugar Twin, and parsley flakes. Mix well to combine. Bring mixture to a boil. Lower heat. Stir in carrots and bacon bits. Cover and simmer for 15 minutes, stirring occasionally.

Each serving equals:

HE: 2⅔ Vegetable • 12 Optional Calories

56 Calories • 0 gm Fat • 3 gm Protein • 11 gm Carbohydrate • 517 mg Sodium • 3 gm Fiber

DIABETIC: 2 Vegetable

Deli-Style Ham and Veggie Pizza

○ Serves 8

1 (11-ounce) can Pillsbury refrigerated crusty French loaf

2 tablespoons prepared mustard

2 full cups (12 ounces) finely diced Dubuque 97% fat free ham or any extra-lean ham

½ cup chopped onion

¾ cup chopped green bell pepper

1½ cups peeled diced fresh tomato

1¼ cups chopped fresh mushrooms

1½ cups (6 ounces) shredded Kraft reduced-fat mozzarella cheese

2 teaspoons dried parsley flakes

Preheat oven to 375 degrees. Spray a rimmed 9-by-13-inch cookie sheet with butter-flavored cooking spray. Unroll French loaf and pat dough into prepared pan and up the sides to form a rim. Bake for 8 minutes or until light golden brown. Remove from oven. Evenly spread mustard over partially baked crust. Layer ham, onion, green pepper, tomato, and mushrooms over crust. Sprinkle mozzarella cheese and parsley flakes evenly over top. Bake for 15 minutes or until crust is golden and cheese is bubbly. Cut into 8 servings.

Each serving equals:

HE: 2 Protein • 1 Bread • 1 Vegetable

193 Calories • 5 gm Fat • 18 gm Protein • 19 gm Carbohydrate • 852 mg Sodium • 1 gm Fiber

DIABETIC: 2 Meat • 1 Starch • 1 Vegetable

Sour Cream Cabbage

● Serves 4 (1 cup)

6 cups shredded cabbage
2 tablespoons water
¼cup Land O Lakes no-fat sour cream
1 tablespoon white vinegar
½ teaspoon lemon pepper

In a large skillet sprayed with butter-flavored cooking spray, combine cabbage and water. Cover and cook on low heat for 8 minutes or just until soft. In a small bowl, combine sour cream, vinegar, and lemon pepper. Add sour cream mixture to undrained cabbage mixture. Mix well to combine. Continue cooking for 2 to 3 minutes or until mixture is heated through.

HINT: Leftovers are as good or better the next day.

Each serving equals:

HE: 3 Vegetable • 15 Optional Calories

40 Calories • 0 gm Fat • 2 gm Protein • 8 gm Carbohydrate • 151 mg Sodium • 2 gm Fiber

DIABETIC: 2 Vegetable

Veggie Coleslaw

☻ Serves 4 (1 full cup)

½ cup Kraft fat-free mayonnaise
¼ teaspoon black pepper
1 teaspoon Italian seasoning
2 cups shredded cabbage
½ cup shredded carrots
¼ cup finely diced green bell pepper
¾ cup shredded zucchini

In a large bowl, combine mayonnaise, black pepper, and Italian seasoning. Add cabbage, carrots, green pepper, and zucchini. Mix well to combine. Cover and refrigerate for at least 20 minutes. Gently stir again just before serving.

HINT: 2½ cups purchased coleslaw mix may be substituted for cabbage and carrots.

Each serving equals:

HE: 1¾ Vegetable • ¼ Slider

36 Calories • 0 gm Fat • 1 gm Protein • 8 gm Carbohydrate • 222 mg Sodium • 1 gm Fiber

DIABETIC: 1 Vegetable • 1 Free Vegetable

Easy Coleslaw

● Serves 4 (¾ cup)

6 tablespoons Land O Lakes no-fat sour cream
2 tablespoons white vinegar
Sugar substitute to equal ¼ cup sugar
½ teaspoon lemon pepper
½ teaspoon prepared mustard
4 cups finely shredded cabbage

In a large bowl, combine sour cream, vinegar, sugar substitute, lemon pepper, and mustard. Add cabbage. Mix well to combine. Cover and refrigerate for at least 20 minutes. Gently stir again just before serving.

Each serving equals:

HE: 2 Vegetable • ¼ Slider • 9 Optional Calories

48 Calories • 0 gm Fat • 2 gm Protein • 10 gm Carbohydrate • 54 mg Sodium • 1 gm Fiber

DIABETIC: 2 Vegetable

Sensational Pineapple Slaw

○ Serves 6 (⅔ cup)

3 cups purchased coleslaw mix

1 cup (one 8-ounce can) pineapple tidbits, packed in fruit juice, drained

⅓ cup (1½ ounces) shredded Kraft reduced-fat Cheddar cheese

½ cup Cool Whip Lite

⅓ cup Kraft fat-free mayonnaise

1 teaspoon lemon juice

In a medium bowl, combine coleslaw mix, pineapple, and Cheddar cheese. In a small bowl, combine Cool Whip Lite, mayonnaise, and lemon juice. Add Cool Whip Lite mixture to coleslaw mixture. Mix well to combine. Cover and refrigerate for at least 20 minutes. Gently stir again just before serving.

HINTS: 1. If you can't find pineapple tidbits, use pineapple chunks and chop coarsely.
2. 2¼ cups shredded cabbage and ½ cup shredded carrots may be used in place of purchased coleslaw mix.

Each serving equals:

HE: 1 Vegetable • ⅓ Protein • ⅓ Fruit • 18 Optional Calories

74 Calories • 2 gm Fat • 3 gm Protein • 11 gm Carbohydrate • 176 mg Sodium • 1 gm Fiber

DIABETIC: 1 Vegetable • ½ Protein • ½ Fruit

Honey Dijon Cukes

● Serves 4 (full ½ cup)

2½ cups unpeeled sliced cucumbers
¼ cup chopped green bell pepper
¼ cup diced onion
¼ cup Kraft Fat Free Honey Dijon Ranch Dressing
2 tablespoons Kraft fat-free mayonnaise
1 teaspoon dried parsley flakes

In a medium bowl, combine cucumbers, green pepper, and onion. In a small bowl, combine Honey Dijon Ranch dressing, mayonnaise, and parsley flakes. Add dressing mixture to cucumber mixture. Mix gently to combine. Cover and refrigerate for at least 20 minutes. Gently stir again just before serving.

Each serving equals:

HE: 1½ Vegetable • ¼ Slider • 10 Optional Calories

36 Calories • 0 gm Fat • 1 gm Protein • 8 gm Carbohydrate • 123 mg Sodium • 1 gm Fiber

DIABETIC: 1½ Vegetable

Broccoli Fruit Slaw

● Serves 6 (⅔ cup)

3 cups purchased broccoli coleslaw mix

1 cup (2 small) unpeeled chopped Red Delicious apples

7 tablespoons raisins

½ cup Kraft fat-free mayonnaise

¼ cup unsweetened orange juice

Sugar substitute to equal 2 tablespoons sugar

In a large bowl, combine broccoli coleslaw mix, apples, and raisins. In a small bowl, combine mayonnaise, orange juice, and sugar substitute. Add mayonnaise mixture to broccoli mixture. Mix gently to combine. Cover and refrigerate for at least 20 minutes. Gently stir again just before serving.

HINT: To plump up raisins without "cooking," place raisins in a glass measuring cup and microwave on HIGH for 20 seconds.

Each serving equals:

HE: 1 Fruit • 1 Vegetable • 15 Optional Calories

80 Calories • 0 gm Fat • 2 gm Protein • 18 gm Carbohydrate • 156 mg Sodium • 2 gm Fiber

DIABETIC: 1 Fruit • 1 Vegetable

Cabbage Patch Slaw

⏺ Serves 4 (¾ cup)

3 cups shredded cabbage
¾ cup shredded carrots
½ cup finely diced celery
¼ cup finely diced onion
½ cup Kraft fat-free mayonnaise
¼ teaspoon lemon pepper
2 teaspoons prepared horseradish
Sugar substitute to equal 2 tablespoons sugar
1 tablespoon white vinegar
1 teaspoon celery seed

In a medium bowl, combine cabbage, carrots, celery, and onion. In a small bowl, combine mayonnaise, lemon pepper, horseradish, sugar substitute, vinegar, and celery seed. Add mayonnaise mixture to cabbage mixture. Mix well to combine. Cover and refrigerate for at least 20 minutes. Gently stir again just before serving.

HINT: 3¾ cups purchased coleslaw mix may be used in place of cabbage and carrots.

Each serving equals:

HE: 2¼ Vegetable • ¼ Slider • 4 Optional Calories

52 Calories • 0 gm Fat • 1 gm Protein • 12 gm Carbohydrate • 245 mg Sodium • 2 Fiber

DIABETIC: 2 Vegetable

Sweet Pickle Coleslaw

◑ Serves 4 (⅔ cup)

2 tablespoons sweet pickle relish
½ teaspoon celery seed
⅓ cup Kraft fat-free mayonnaise
3 cups purchased coleslaw mix

In a medium bowl, combine sweet pickle relish, celery seed, and mayonnaise. Add coleslaw mix. Mix well to combine. Cover and refrigerate for at least 20 minutes. Gently stir again just before serving.

HINT: 2½ cups shredded cabbage and ½ cup shredded carrots may be used instead of purchased coleslaw mix.

Each serving equals:

HE: 1½ Vegetable • 14 Optional Calories

40 Calories • 0 gm Fat • 1 gm Protein • 9 gm Carbohydrate •
206 mg Sodium • 1 gm Fiber

DIABETIC: 1½ Vegetable

Southern Belle Slaw

❂ Serves 4 (full ½ cup)

2 cups purchased coleslaw mix
1 cup (one 11-ounce can) mandarin oranges, rinsed and drained
2 tablespoons (½ ounce) chopped pecans
½ cup Kraft fat-free mayonnaise
2 tablespoons Cary's Sugar Free Maple Syrup

In a large bowl, combine coleslaw mix, mandarin oranges, and pecans. In a small bowl, combine mayonnaise and maple syrup. Add mayonnaise mixture to coleslaw mixture. Toss gently to combine. Cover and refrigerate for at least 20 minutes. Gently stir again just before serving.

HINT: 1½ cups shredded cabbage and ½ cup shredded carrots may be used in place of purchased coleslaw mix.

Each serving equals:

HE: 1 Vegetable • ½ Fat • ½ Fruit • ¼ Slider • 5 Optional Calories

78 Calories • 2 gm Fat • 1 gm Protein • 14 gm Carbohydrate • 233 mg Sodium • 1 gm Fiber

DIABETIC: 1 Vegetable • ½ Fat • ½ Fruit

Main Dishes

Does cooking seem like work to you, a four-letter word you'd just as soon avoid? Well, these dishes are so easy to prepare and require so little effort, you'll earn a reputation as a smart cook—a four-letter-word you might like a lot! Why not serve my Terrific Taco Toss tonight, or win fans with Easy Italian Meat Loaf in just minutes?

Luncheon Fruit Pita

Never thought about eating fruit in a sandwich? Well, this crunchy cream cheese blend is truly luscious and flavorful, and works perfectly when stuffed into a pita for a fast lunch!　❂　Serves 4

½ cup (4 ounces) Philadelphia fat-free cream cheese

¼ teaspoon coconut extract

1 tablespoon Brown Sugar Twin

1 cup (2 small) unpeeled, cored and chopped Red Delicious apples

1 cup (one 8-ounce can) crushed pineapple, packed in fruit juice, drained

¼ cup (1 ounce) chopped walnuts

½ cup finely shredded lettuce

2 pita rounds, cut in half

1 tablespoon + 1 teaspoon flaked coconut

In a medium bowl, stir cream cheese with a spoon until soft. Add coconut extract and Brown Sugar Twin. Mix well to combine. Stir in apples, pineapple, and walnuts. For each sandwich, place about 2 tablespoons shredded lettuce in a pita half, spoon about ½ cup fruit mixture over lettuce, and top with 1 teaspoon coconut. Serve at once or refrigerate until ready to serve.

HINT:　To make opening pita rounds easier, place pita halves on a paper towel and microwave on HIGH for 10 seconds. Remove and gently press open.

Each serving equals:

HE: 1 Bread • 1 Fruit • ¾ Protein • ½ Fat • ¼ Vegetable • 1 Optional Calorie

213 Calories • 5 gm Fat • 8 gm Protein • 34 gm Carbohydrate • 337 mg Sodium • 45 mg Calcium • 2 gm Fiber

DIABETIC: 1 Starch • 1 Fruit • 1 Fat • ½ Meat

Cheesy Rice-Corn Skillet

Serves 6 (1 cup)

1½ cups finely chopped celery
½ cup chopped onion
2 cups cold cooked rice
2 cups frozen whole kernel corn
⅔ cup Carnation Nonfat Dry Milk Powder
1 cup water
1½ cups (6 ounces) shredded Kraft reduced-fat Cheddar cheese
¼ cup (¾ ounce) grated Kraft fat-free Parmesan cheese
2 teaspoons dried parsley flakes
¼ teaspoon lemon pepper

In a large skillet sprayed with butter-flavored cooking spray, sauté celery and onion for 6 to 8 minutes or until just tender. Stir in rice and corn. In a small bowl, combine dry milk powder and water. Add milk mixture to the celery mixture. Mix well to combine. Stir Cheddar cheese, Parmesan cheese, parsley flakes, and lemon pepper into celery mixture. Lower heat and simmer for 10 minutes, stirring occasionally.

HINT: 1⅓ cups dry rice usually cooks to about 2 cups.

Each serving equals:

HE: 1½ Protein • 1⅓ Bread • ⅔ Vegetable • ⅓ Skim Milk

220 Calories • 4 gm Fat • 15 gm Protein • 31 gm Carbohydrate • 338 mg Sodium • 3 gm Fiber

DIABETIC: 1½ Meat • 1½ Starch • ½ Vegetable

Mexican Onion and Spaghetti Skillet

Serves 4 (1 cup)

3 cups sliced onion

1½ cups (one 12-fluid-ounce can) Carnation Evaporated Skim Milk

3 tablespoons all-purpose flour

¼ teaspoon lemon pepper

1 teaspoon dried parsley flakes

¾ cup (3 ounces) shredded Kraft reduced-fat Cheddar cheese

½ cup chunky salsa (mild, medium, or hot)

1½ cups hot cooked spaghetti, rinsed and drained

In a large skillet sprayed with butter-flavored cooking spray, sauté onion for 10 minutes or until tender. In a covered jar, combine evaporated skim milk, flour, lemon pepper, and parsley flakes. Shake well to blend. Pour milk mixture into skillet with onion. Add Cheddar cheese, salsa, and spaghetti. Mix well to combine. Lower heat and simmer for 10 minutes, stirring often.

Each serving equals:

HE: 1¾ Vegetable • 1 Protein • 1 Bread • ¾ Skim Milk

---

264 Calories • 4 gm Fat • 18 gm Protein • 39 gm Carbohydrate • 389 mg Sodium • 3 gm Fiber

---

DIABETIC: 1½ Vegetable • 1 Meat • 1 Starch • 1 Skim Milk

Macaroni "Lasagna" Skillet

● Serves 4

1¾ cups (one 15-ounce can) Hunt's Chunky Tomato Sauce

¼ teaspoon dried minced garlic

1 teaspoon Italian seasoning

1 teaspoon dried parsley flakes

¼ teaspoon black pepper

1 cup fat-free cottage cheese

1½ cup (¾ ounce) shredded Kraft reduced-fat mozzarella cheese☆

¼ cup (¾ ounce) grated Kraft fat-free Parmesan cheese

2 cups hot cooked macaroni, rinsed and drained

In a large skillet sprayed with olive oil-flavored cooking spray, combine tomato sauce, garlic, Italian seasoning, parsley flakes, and black pepper. Bring mixture to a boil. Add cottage cheese, 1 cup mozzarella cheese and Parmesan cheese. Mix well to combine. Continue cooking for 5 minutes or until the cheeses begin to melt, stirring often. Stir in macaroni. Evenly sprinkle remaining ½ cup mozzarella cheese over top. Lower heat, cover, and simmer for 5 minutes or until mozzarella cheese melts. Divide into 4 (1-cup) servings.

HINT: 1⅓ cups uncooked macaroni usually cooks to about 2 cups.

Each serving equals:

HE: 2¾ Protein • 1¾ Vegetable • 1 Bread

282 Calories • 6 gm Fat • 28 gm Protein • 29 gm Carbohydrate • 976 mg Sodium • 1 gm Fiber

DIABETIC: 3 Meat • 1½ Vegetable • 1½ Starch

El Grande Potato Bake

● Serves 4

1²⁄₃ cups water

¼ cup finely chopped onion

1 cup (3 ounces) instant potato flakes

⅓ cup Carnation Nonfat Dry Milk Powder

1 teaspoon taco seasoning mix

10 ounces (one 16-ounce can) red kidney beans, rinsed and drained

1¾ cups (one 14½ ounce can) stewed tomatoes, coarsely chopped and undrained

¾ cup (3 ounces) shredded Kraft reduced-fat Cheddar cheese

1 teaspoon dried parsley flakes

Preheat oven to 350 degrees. Spray an 8-by-8-inch baking dish with olive oil-flavored cooking spray. In a medium saucepan, combine water and onion. Cook over medium heat until mixture starts to boil. Remove from heat. Stir in potato flakes, dry milk powder, and taco seasoning mix. Add kidney beans. Mix well to combine. Spread mixture evenly into prepared baking dish. Evenly spread undrained stewed tomatoes over potato mixture. Sprinkle Cheddar cheese and parsley flakes over top. Bake for 20 minutes. Place baking dish on a wire rack and let set for 5 minutes. Divide into 4 servings.

Each serving equals:

HE: 2¼ Protein • 1 Bread • 1 Vegetable • ¼ Skim Milk

211 Calories • 3 gm Fat • 14 gm Protein • 32 gm Carbohydrate • 493 mg Sodium • 7 mg Fiber

DIABETIC: 2 Starch • 1½ Meat • 1 Vegetable

Frankfurter Green Bean Bake

● Serves 4

½ cup chopped onion

8 ounces Healthy Choice 97% fat-free frankfurters, diced

4 cups (two 16-ounce cans) cut green beans, rinsed and drained

1¾ cups (one 15-ounce can) Hunt's Chunky Tomato Sauce

1 teaspoon prepared mustard

2 tablespoons Brown Sugar Twin

¼ teaspoon black pepper

Preheat oven to 350 degrees. Spray an 8-by-8-inch baking dish with butter-flavored cooking spray. In a large skillet sprayed with butter-flavored cooking spray, sauté onion and frankfurters for 5 minutes or until onion is tender. Stir in green beans and tomato sauce. Add mustard, Brown Sugar Twin, and black pepper. Mix well to combine. Pour mixture into prepared baking dish. Bake for 20 to 25 minutes. Place baking dish on a wire rack and let set for 5 minutes. Divide into 4 servings.

HINT: 1½ cups (8 ounces) diced Dubuque 97% fat free ham or any extra-lean ham may be used in place of frankfurters.

Each serving equals:

HE: 4 Vegetable • 1⅓ Protein • 2 Optional Calories

129 Calories • 1 gm Fat • 11 gm Protein • 19 gm Carbohydrate • 995 mg Sodium • 2 gm Fiber

DIABETIC: 4 Vegetable • 1 Meat *or* 1 Starch • 1 Vegetable • 1 Meat

Zucchini Pastrami Pasta Toss

● Serves 4 (full 1 cup)

2 cups unpeeled sliced zucchini

2 (2.5-ounce) packages Carl Buddig lean pastrami

1¾ cups (one 15-ounce can) Hunt's Chunky Tomato Sauce

1½ teaspoons Italian seasoning

¼ cup (¾ ounce) grated Kraft fat-free Parmesan cheese

2 cups hot cooked rotini pasta, rinsed and drained

In a large skillet sprayed with olive oil-flavored cooking spray, sauté zucchini and pastrami for 5 minutes or until lightly browned. Add tomato sauce and Italian seasoning. Mix well to combine. Stir in Parmesan cheese and rotini pasta. Lower heat and simmer for 10 minutes or until mixture is heated through, stirring occasionally.

HINTS: 1. 1½ cups uncooked rotini pasta usually cooks to about 2 cups.

2. Garden Variety Rotini pasta works great.

Each serving equals:

HE: 2¾ Vegetable • 1½ Protein • 1 Bread

203 Calories • 3 gm Fat • 14 gm Protein • 30 gm Carbohydrate • 1060 mg Sodium • 2 gm Fiber

DIABETIC: 3 Vegetable • 1½ Meat • 1 Starch

Barbeque Tuna and Noodles

● Serves 4 (1 cup)

½ cup chopped green bell pepper

½ cup chopped onion

1 teaspoon Worcestershire sauce

1¾ cups (one 15-ounce can) Hunt's Chunky Tomato Sauce

1 tablespoon Brown Sugar Twin

1 teaspoon chili seasoning mix

1 tablespoon white vinegar

1 (6-ounce) can white tuna, packed in water, drained and flaked

2 cups hot cooked noodles, rinsed and drained

In a large skillet sprayed with butter-flavored cooking spray, sauté green pepper and onion for 6 to 8 minutes or until tender. Stir in Worcestershire sauce, tomato sauce, Brown Sugar Twin, chili seasoning mix, and vinegar. Add tuna and noodles. Mix well to combine. Lower heat and simmer for 10 minutes or until mixture is heated through, stirring occasionally.

HINT: 1¾ cups uncooked noodles usually cooks to about 2 cups.

Each serving equals:

HE: 2¼ Vegetable • ¾ Protein • 1 Bread • 1 Optional Calorie

194 Calories • 2 gm Fat • 16 gm Protein • 28 gm Carbohydrate • 864 mg Sodium • 2 gm Fiber

DIABETIC: 1½ Vegetable • 1½ Meat • 1 Starch

Tuna Potato Bake

● Serves 4

1⅔ cups water

1⅓ cups (3 ounces) instant potato flakes

⅓ cup Carnation Nonfat Dry Milk Powder

¾ cup Yoplait plain fat-free yogurt

2 tablespoons Kraft fat-free mayonnaise

¼ teaspoon black pepper

1 teaspoon dried parsley flakes

1 teaspoon chili seasoning mix

1 (9½ ounce) can white tuna, packed in water, drained and flaked

¾ cup (3 ounces) shredded Kraft reduced-fat Cheddar cheese

½ cup chopped green bell pepper

Spray an 8-by-8-inch glass baking dish with butter flavored cooking spray. In an 8-cup glass measuring bowl, microwave water on HIGH (100% power) until water starts to boil, about 2 minutes. Add potato flakes and dry milk powder. Mix well to combine. Let cool for 2 to 3 minutes. Stir in yogurt, mayonnaise, black pepper, parsley flakes, and chili seasoning mix. Add tuna, Cheddar cheese, and green pepper. Mix well to combine. Spread mixture into prepared baking dish. Cover with waxed paper. Microwave on HIGH for 6 minutes, turning after 3 minutes. Place baking dish on a wire rack and let set for 3 to 5 minutes. Divide into 4 servings.

Each serving equals:

HE: 2 Protein • 1 Bread • ½ Skim Milk • ¼ Vegetable • 5 Optional Calories

236 Calories • 4 gm Fat • 29 gm Protein • 21 gm Carbohydrate • 525 mg Sodium • 1 gm Fiber

DIABETIC: 3 Meat • 1 Starch • ½ Skim Milk

Easy Fish Creole

♥ Serves 4

½ cup chopped onion
¾ cup chopped celery
½ cup chopped green bell pepper
1¾ cups (one 14½ ounce can) stewed tomatoes, coarsely chopped and undrained
½ teaspoon dried minced garlic
1 tablespoon Brown Sugar Twin
16 ounces white fish, cut into 16 pieces
2 cups hot cooked rice

In a large skillet sprayed with butter-flavored cooking spray, sauté onion, celery, and green pepper for 10 minutes or until tender. Stir in undrained stewed tomatoes, garlic, and Brown Sugar Twin. Add fish. Mix gently to combine. Lower heat, cover and simmer for 20 minutes, stirring occasionally. For each serving, place ½ cup rice on a plate and spoon about 1 full cup fish mixture over top.

HINT: 1⅓ cups uncooked rice usually cooks to about 2 cups.

Each serving equals:

HE: 1¾ Vegetable • 1½ Protein • 1 Bread • 1 Optional Calorie

198 Calories • 2 gm Fat • 25 gm Protein • 20 gm Carbohydrate • 658 mg Sodium

DIABETIC: 3 Meat • 1 Vegetable • 1 Starch

Baked Fish Italian

◐ Serves 4

6 tablespoons (1½ ounces) dried fine bread crumbs
2 teaspoons Italian seasoning
⅓ cup Kraft Fat Free Italian Dressing
16 ounces white fish, cut into 4 pieces

Preheat oven to 350 degrees. Spray an 8-by-8-inch baking dish with butter-flavored cooking spray. In a sealed sandwich bag, combine bread crumbs and Italian seasoning. Pour Italian dressing into a dipping dish. Coat fish pieces in dressing, then place in sandwich bag, one piece at a time, and shake well to coat. Place fish pieces in prepared baking dish. Bake for 15 minutes or until fish flakes easily. Lightly spray tops of fish with butter-flavored cooking spray. Serve at once.

Each serving equals:

HE: 1½ Protein • ½ Bread • 5 Optional Calories

135 Calories • 3 gm Fat • 18 gm Protein • 9 gm Carbohydrate • 170 mg Sodium • 0 gm Fiber

DIABETIC: 3 Meat • ½ Starch

Fiesta Burgers

◑ Serves 6 (⅓ cup filling)

16 ounces ground 90% lean turkey or beef
½ cup chopped onion
½ cup chopped green bell pepper
1 (10¾ ounce) can Healthy Request Tomato Soup
2 teaspoons chili seasoning mix
¼ teaspoon black pepper
6 reduced-calorie hamburger buns

In a large skillet sprayed with olive oil-flavored cooking spray, brown meat, onion, and green pepper. Add tomato soup, chili seasoning mix, and black pepper. Mix well to combine. Lower heat and simmer for 10 minutes, stirring occasionally. Serve on hamburger buns.

Each serving equals:

HE: 2 Protein • 1 Bread • ⅓ Vegetable • ¼ Slider •
10 Optional Calories

228 Calories • 8 gm Fat • 16 gm Protein • 23 gm Carbohydrate •
425 mg Sodium • 2 gm Fiber

DIABETIC: 2 Meat • 1½ Starch

Tex-Mex Skillet Hash

● Serves 4 (1 full cup)

8 ounces ground 90% lean turkey or beef
½ cup chopped onion
½ cup chopped green bell pepper
1¾ cups (one 15-ounce can) Hunt's Chunky Tomato Sauce
10 ounces (one 16-ounce can) red kidney beans, rinsed and drained
2 teaspoons chili seasoning mix
1 tablespoon Brown Sugar Twin
1½ cups hot cooked rice

In a large skillet sprayed with olive oil-flavored cooking spray, brown meat, onion, and green pepper. Stir in tomato sauce, kidney beans, chili seasoning mix, and Brown Sugar Twin. Add rice. Mix well to combine. Lower heat and simmer for 10 minutes or until mixture is heated through, stirring occasionally.

HINT: 1 cup uncooked rice usually cooks to about 1½ cups.

Each serving equals:

HE: 2¾ Protein • 2¼ Vegetable • ¾ Bread

241 Calories • 5 gm Fat • 17 gm Protein • 32 gm Carbohydrate • 757 mg Sodium • 5 gm Fiber

DIABETIC: 2 Meat • 2 Starch • 1 Vegetable

Crunchy Loose Meat Sandwiches

☻ Serves 8 (scant ½ cup filling)

16 ounces ground 90% lean turkey or beef
½ cup chopped onion
2 cups purchased coleslaw mix
1¾ cups (one 15-ounce can) Hunt's Chunky Tomato Sauce
1 teaspoon prepared mustard
1 teaspoon taco seasoning
¼ teaspoon black pepper
1 tablespoon Brown Sugar Twin
8 reduced-calorie hamburger buns

In a large skillet sprayed with butter-flavored cooking spray, brown meat and onion. Add coleslaw mix. Mix well to combine. Continue cooking for 5 minutes, stirring often. Stir in tomato sauce, mustard, taco seasoning, black pepper, and Brown Sugar Twin. Lower heat and simmer for 10 minutes, stirring occasionally. Serve on hamburger buns.

HINT: 1½ cups shredded cabbage and ½ cup shredded carrots may be used in place of purchased coleslaw mix.

Each serving equals:

HE: 1½ Protein • 1½ Vegetable • 1 Bread • 1 Optional Calorie

182 Calories • 6 gm Fat • 13 gm Protein • 19 gm Carbohydrate • 577 mg Sodium • 1 gm Fiber

DIABETIC: 1½ Meat • 1 Vegetable • 1 Starch

Saucy "Faux" Steaks

● Serves 6

16 ounces ground 90% lean turkey or beef

6 tablespoons (1½ ounces) dried fine bread crumbs

¼ cup finely chopped onion

½ cup Heinz Light Harvest or Healthy Choice ketchup☆

1¾ cups (one 14½ ounce can) stewed tomatoes, undrained

In a large bowl, combine meat, bread crumbs, onion, and ¼ cup ketchup. Mix well to combine. Using a ⅓-cup measure as a guide, form mixture into 6 patties. Place patties in a large skillet sprayed with butter-flavored cooking spray. Brown about 3 minutes on each side. In a small bowl, combine undrained stewed tomatoes and remaining ¼ cup ketchup. Pour stewed tomato mixture evenly over browned meat. Lower heat, cover, and simmer for 15 minutes. When serving, evenly spoon sauce over "steaks."

Each serving equals:

HE: 2 Protein • ⅔ Vegetable • ⅓ Bread • ½ Slider

175 Calories • 7 gm Fat • 15 gm Protein • 13 gm Carbohydrate • 467 mg Sodium • 1 gm Fiber

DIABETIC: 2 Meat • 1 Vegetable • ½ Starch

Dill Cheeseburger Meat Loaf

● Serves 6

16 ounces ground 90% lean turkey or beef

½ cup + 1 tablespoon (2¼ ounces) dried fine bread crumbs

½ cup dill pickle relish

¾ cup (3 ounces) shredded Kraft reduced-fat Cheddar cheese

½ cup chopped onion

1 (10¾ ounce) can Healthy Request Tomato Soup☆

1 tablespoon Brown Sugar Twin

In a large bowl, combine meat, bread crumbs, pickle relish, Cheddar cheese, onion, and ¼ cup tomato soup. Mix well to combine. Place a small custard cup in center of deep-dish 10-inch glass pie plate or use a microwave ring mold. Evenly spread meat mixture into prepared pie plate. In a small bowl, combine remaining ¾ cup tomato soup and Brown Sugar Twin. Evenly spoon soup mixture over top of meat mixture. Microwave on HIGH (100% power) for 8 minutes. Turn dish and continue microwaving on HIGH for 8 minutes. Place baking dish on a wire rack and let set for 5 minutes. Cut into 6 servings.

Each serving equals:

HE: 2⅔ Protein • ½ Bread • ⅓ Vegetable • ¼ Slider •
11 Optional Calories

204 Calories • 8 gm Fat • 18 gm Protein • 15 gm Carbohydrate •
620 mg Sodium • 1 gm Fiber

DIABETIC: 2½ Meat • ½ Starch • ½ Vegetable

Onion Meat Loaf

● Serves 6

16 ounces ground 90% lean turkey or beef

6 slices reduced-calorie white bread, made into soft crumbs

1 cup chopped onion

1 cup (one 8-ounce can) Hunt's Tomato Sauce☆

1 tablespoon Brown Sugar Twin

2 teaspoons prepared mustard

¼ teaspoon black pepper

In a large bowl, combine meat, bread crumbs, onion, ⅓ cup tomato sauce, Brown Sugar Twin, mustard, and black pepper. Mix well to combine. Place a small custard cup in center of deep-dish 10-inch glass pie plate or use a microwave ring mold. Evenly spread meat mixture into prepared pie plate. Spoon remaining ⅔ cup tomato sauce evenly over top of meat mixture. Microwave on HIGH (100% power) for 8 minutes. Turn dish half turn and continue microwaving on HIGH for an additional 8 minutes. Place pie plate on a wire rack and let set for 5 minutes. Cut into 6 servings.

Each serving equals:

HE: 2 Protein • 1 Vegetable • ½ Bread • 1 Optional Calorie

170 Calories • 6 gm Fat • 17 gm Protein • 12 gm Carbohydrate • 450 mg Sodium • 0 gm Fiber

DIABETIC: 2 Meat • 1 Vegetable • ½ Starch

Quick Turkey-'n'-Biscuits

● Serves 6

1½ cups (8-ounces) diced cooked turkey breast

1 (10¾ ounce) can Healthy Request Cream of Chicken Soup

1 teaspoon dried onion flakes

1 teaspoon dried parsley flakes

1 cup (one 8-ounce can) sliced carrots, rinsed and drained

1 cup (one 8-ounce can) cut green beans, rinsed and drained

1 (7.5-ounce) can Pillsbury refrigerated buttermilk biscuits

Preheat oven to 400 degrees. Spray an 8-by-8-inch baking dish with butter-flavored cooking spray. In a large bowl, combine turkey, chicken soup, onion flakes, and parsley flakes. Mix well to combine. Stir in carrots and green beans. Spread turkey mixture into prepared baking dish. Separate and cut each biscuit into 4 pieces. Evenly sprinkle biscuit pieces over top of turkey mixture. Lightly spray tops of biscuit pieces with butter-flavored cooking spray. Bake for 15 minutes or until biscuits are golden brown. Place baking dish on a wire rack and let set for 2 to 3 minutes. Divide into 6 servings.

HINT: IF you don't have leftovers, purchase a chunk of cooked turkey breast from your local deli.

Each serving equals:

HE: 1⅓ Protein • 1¼ Bread • ⅔ Vegetable • ¼ Slider • 10 Optional Calories

---

196 Calories • 4 gm Fat • 16 gm Protein • 24 gm Carbohydrate • 567 mg Sodium • 2 gm Fiber

---

DIABETIC: 1½ Meat • 1 Starch • 1 Vegetable

Veggie Turkey and Stuffing Skillet

◑ Serves 6 (1 cup)

2 cups (one 16-ounce can) Healthy Request Chicken Broth

1 (16-ounce) package frozen carrot, broccoli, and cauliflower blend

1 (6-ounce) package Stove Top Chicken Flavored Stuffing Mix

1 (10¾ ounce) can Healthy Request Cream of Chicken Soup

¾ cup Yoplait plain fat-free yogurt

⅓ cup Carnation Nonfat Dry Milk Powder

1 teaspoon cornstarch

1½ cups (8 ounces) chopped cooked turkey breast

In a large skillet, combine chicken broth, frozen vegetables, and seasoning packet from stuffing mix. Bring mixture to a boil. Lower heat and simmer for 5 minutes. Stir in dry stuffing mix. In a small bowl, combine chicken soup, yogurt, dry milk powder, and cornstarch. Add soup mixture to stuffing mixture. Mix well to combine. Fold in turkey. Lower heat and simmer for 8 to 10 minutes, stirring occasionally.

HINTS: 1. 1 cup frozen carrots, 1 cup frozen broccoli, and 1 cup frozen cauliflower may be used in place of blended vegetables.
2. If you don't have leftovers, purchase a chunk of cooked turkey breast from your local deli.

Each serving equals:

HE: 1⅓ Protein • 1⅓ Bread • 1 Vegetable • ⅓ Skim Milk • ¼ Slider • 13 Optional Calories

267 Calories • 3 gm Fat • 21 gm Protein • 39 gm Carbohydrate • 928 mg Sodium • 2 gm Fiber

DIABETIC: 1½ Starch • 1 Meat • 1 Vegetable

Easy Glazed Chicken

○ Serves 4

16 ounces skinned and boned uncooked chicken breast, cut into 4 pieces
1 tablespoon dried onion flakes
¼ cup Kraft Fat Free French Dressing
¼ cup apricot spreadable fruit spread
2 tablespoons water
1 teaspoon dried parsley flakes

In a large skillet sprayed with butter-flavored cooking spray, brown chicken pieces for 3 minutes on each side. In a small bowl, combine onion flakes, French dressing, fruit spread, water, and parsley flakes. Spoon dressing mixture evenly over chicken pieces. Lower heat, cover, and simmer for 15 minutes or until chicken is tender. When serving, evenly spoon sauce over chicken pieces.

Each serving equals:

HE: 3 Protein • 1 Fruit • ¼ Slider • 5 Optional Calories

244 Calories • 4 gm Fat • 35 gm Protein • 17 gm Carbohydrate • 219 mg Sodium • 0 gm Fiber

DIABETIC: 3 Meat • 1 Fruit

Mex-Italian Chicken Skillet

⭘ Serves 4 (1 cup)

3 tablespoons all-purpose flour

1 teaspoon Italian seasoning

16 ounces skinned and boned uncooked chicken breast, cut into 24 pieces

2 tablespoons skim milk

1¾ cups (one 15-ounce can) Hunt's Chunky Tomato Sauce

½ cup chunky salsa (mild, medium, or hot)

1½ cups hot cooked spaghetti, rinsed and drained

¼ cup (¾ ounce) grated Kraft fat-free Parmesan cheese

In a saucer, combine flour and Italian seasoning. Dip chicken pieces in skim milk, then into flour mixture. (Reserve any remaining flour.) Place chicken pieces in a large skillet sprayed with olive oil-flavored cooking spray. Brown chicken pieces for 4 minutes, stirring often. In a medium bowl, combine tomato sauce, salsa, and any remaining flour mixture. Add sauce mixture. Mix well to combine. Lower heat, cover and simmer for 10 minutes, stirring occasionally. Stir in spaghetti and Parmesan cheese. Continue cooking for 5 minutes or until mixture is heated through, stirring often.

HINT: Full 1 cup uncooked spaghetti usually cooks to about 1½ cups.

Each serving equals:

HE: 3¼ Protein • 2 Vegetable • 1 Bread • 3 Optional Calories

292 Calories • 4 gm Fat • 36 gm Protein • 28 gm Carbohydrate • 968 mg Sodium • 2 gm Fiber

DIABETIC: 3 Meat • 2 Vegetable • 1 Starch

Quickie Chicken Rice Skillet

● Serves 4 (1 full cup)

1 (10¾ ounce) can Healthy Request Cream of Chicken Soup
1 cup skim milk
2 teaspoons reduced-sodium soy sauce
1½ cups (8 ounces) diced cooked chicken breast
½ cup frozen peas
¼ cup canned chopped pimientos
¼ teaspoon black pepper
1 cup (3 ounces) uncooked instant rice

In a large skillet, combine chicken soup, skim milk, and soy sauce. Stir in chicken, peas, pimientos, and black pepper. Bring mixture to a boil. Add rice. Mix well to combine. Remove from heat, cover, and let set for 5 minutes. Stir again just before serving.

HINT: If you don't have leftovers, purchase a chunk of cooked chicken breast from your local deli.

Each serving equals:

HE: 2 Protein • 1 Bread • ¼ Skim Milk • ½ Slider •
5 Optional Calories

216 Calories • 4 gm Fat • 23 gm Protein • 22 gm Carbohydrate •
414 mg Sodium • 1 gm Fiber

DIABETIC: 2 Meat • 2 Starch

Grilled Cheese and Ham Sandwich

🢅 Serves 4

¼ cup Kraft fat-free mayonnaise
1 teaspoon prepared mustard
8 slices reduced-calorie white bread
1 (6-ounce) package Healthy Choice sliced 97% fat-free ham
4 (¾ ounce) slices Kraft reduced-fat American cheese

Spray a large skillet with butter-flavored cooking spray. In a small bowl, combine mayonnaise and mustard. Spread mayonnaise mixture evenly over 4 slices of bread. Evenly divide and layer ham slices over top and arrange 1 slice American cheese and remaining slices of bread on top of each. Place sandwiches in skillet. Cover and brown on medium heat, for about 3 minutes. Lightly spray tops of bread with butter-flavored cooking spray and flip sandwiches over. Cover skillet again and brown just until cheese is melted, about 1 to 2 minutes. Serve at once.

HINT: Bread browns quickly, so watch closely.

Each serving equals:

HE: 2 Protein • 1 Bread • 10 Optional Calories

167 Calories • 3 gm Fat • 17 gm Protein • 18 gm Carbohydrate • 747 mg Sodium • 0 gm Fiber

DIABETIC: 2 Meat • 1 Starch

Creamy Chicken and Vegetable Skillet

☻ Serves 4 (1 cup)

3½ cups purchased stir-fry vegetables (fresh or frozen)
⅓ cup water
1 full cup (6 ounces) diced cooked chicken breast
1 (10¾ ounce) can Healthy Request Cream of Chicken Soup
¼ teaspoon black pepper

In a large skillet sprayed with butter-flavored cooking spray, sauté vegetables for 5 minutes, stirring often. Stir in water. Lower heat, cover, and simmer 5 minutes. Add chicken, chicken soup, and black pepper. Mix well to combine. Continue cooking for 5 minutes or until mixture is heated through, stirring occasionally.

HINTS: 1. If you don't want to use purchased stir-fry vegetables, use any vegetable combination of your choice.
2. If you don't have leftovers, purchase a chunk of cooked chicken breast from your local deli.

Each serving equals:

HE: 1¾ Vegetable • 1½ Protein • ½ Slider • 5 Optional Calories

142 Calories • 2 gm Fat • 13 gm Protein • 18 gm Carbohydrate • 396 mg Sodium • 3 gm Fiber

DIABETIC: 2 Vegetable • 1½ Meat • ½ Starch

BBQ Ham-Macaroni Salad

◐ Serves 6 (⅔ cup)

2 cups cold-cooked elbow macaroni, rinsed and drained

1 cup frozen peas, thawed

1 full cup (6 ounces) diced Dubuque 97% fat-free ham or any extra-lean ham

½ cup Kraft fat-free mayonnaise

3 tablespoons Healthy Choice BBQ sauce

1 teaspoon dried parsley flakes

In a large bowl, combine macaroni, peas, and ham. In a small bowl, combine mayonnaise, BBQ sauce, and parsley flakes. Add mayonnaise mixture to macaroni mixture. Mix gently to combine. Cover and refrigerate for at least 20 minutes. Gently stir again just before serving.

HINTS: 1. 1⅓ cups uncooked macaroni usually cooks to about 2 cups.

2. To Thaw peas, place in a colander and rinse under hot water for one minute.

Each serving equals:

HE: 1 Bread • ⅔ Protein • ¼ Slider • 3 Optional Calories

129 Calories • 1 gm Fat • 8 gm Protein • 22 gm Carbohydrate • 498 mg Sodium • 2 gm Fiber

DIABETIC: 1½ Starch • ½ Meat

Macaroni-Ham Skillet

○ Serves 6

½ cup chopped onion

1 full cup (6 ounces) diced Dubuque 97% fat-free ham or any extra-lean ham

½ cup (one 2.5-ounce jar) sliced mushrooms, drained

3 cups hot cooked elbow macaroni, rinsed and drained

1 (10¾ ounce) can Healthy Request Cream of Mushroom Soup

½ cup skim milk

1 teaspoon dried parsley flakes

¼ cup (¾ ounce) grated Kraft fat-free Parmesan cheese

3 (¾ ounce) slices Kraft reduced-fat Swiss cheese

In a large skillet sprayed with butter-flavored cooking spray, sauté onion and ham for 5 minutes or until onion is tender. Stir in mushrooms and macaroni. Add mushroom soup, skim milk, parsley flakes, and Parmesan cheese. Mix well to combine. Lower heat and simmer for 5 minutes. Cut Swiss cheese slices in half. Evenly space cheese pieces over top of macaroni mixture. Cover and continue simmering for 2 to 3 minutes or until cheese melts. Divide into 6 (1-cup) servings.

HINT: 2 cups uncooked macaroni usually cooks to about 3 cups.

Each serving equals:

HE: 2 Protein • 1 Bread • ⅓ Vegetable • ¼ Slider • 15 Optional Calories

191 Calories • 3 gm Fat • 12 gm Protein • 29 gm Carbohydrate • 573 mg Sodium • 2 gm Fiber

DIABETIC: 2 Starch • 1½ Meat

Busy Day Pork Casserole

● Serves 4

4 (4-ounce) lean tenderized pork tenderloins

1 (10¾ ounce) can Healthy Request Cream of Mushroom Soup

½ cup (one 2.5-ounce jar) sliced mushrooms, drained

2 cups (one 16-ounce can) cut green beans, rinsed and drained

¼ teaspoon lemon pepper

3 tablespoons (¾ ounce) dried fine bread crumbs

Preheat oven to 375 degrees. Spray an 8-by-8-inch baking dish with butter-flavored cooking spray. Lightly brown tenderloins in a large skillet sprayed with butter-flavored cooking spray. Place tenderloins in prepared baking dish. In same skillet, combine mushroom soup, mushrooms, green beans, and lemon pepper. Cook for 2 to 3 minutes, stirring often. Pour soup mixture evenly over browned meat. Sprinkle bread crumbs evenly over the top. Bake for 20 minutes, or until pork is tender. Divide into 4 servings.

Each serving equals:

HE: 3 Protein • 1¼ Vegetable • ¼ Bread • ½ Slider •
1 Optional Calorie

227 Calories • 7 gm Fat • 27 gm Protein • 14 gm Carbohydrate •
516 mg Sodium • 1 gm Fiber

DIABETIC: 3 Meat • 1 Vegetable • ½ Starch

Tomato Pork Stroganoff

○ Serves 4 (1 cup)

1 cup chopped onion
½ cup (one 2.5-ounce jar) sliced mushrooms, drained
1 full cup (6 ounces) diced lean cooked roast pork
1 (10¾ ounce) can Healthy Request Tomato Soup
1 teaspoon dried parsley flakes
¼ teaspoon black pepper
¼ cup Land O Lakes no-fat sour cream
2 cups hot cooked noodles, rinsed and drained

In a large skillet sprayed with butter-flavored cooking spray, sauté onion for 5 minutes or until tender. Add mushrooms, roast pork, tomato soup, parsley flakes, and black pepper. Mix well to combine. Stir in sour cream and noodles. Lower heat and simmer for 5 minutes or until mixture is heated through, stirring often.

HINTS: 1. If you don't have leftovers, purchase a chunk of cooked roast pork from your local deli.
2. Lean roast beef may be used in place of pork.
3. 1¾ cups uncooked noodles usually cooks to about 2 cups.

Each serving equals:

HE: 1½ Protein • 1 Bread • ¾ Vegetable • ¾ Slider

278 Calories • 6 gm Fat • 18 gm Protein • 38 mg Carbohydrate • 428 mg Sodium • 6 gm Fiber

DIABETIC: 2 Starch • 1½ Meat • 1 Vegetable

Hot Roast Beef Sandwiches

○ Serves 4

1 (6-ounce)-package Healthy Choice sliced 97% fat free roast beef

1 (12-ounce) jar Heinz Fat Free Beef Gravy

1⅔ cups hot water

1⅓ cups (3 ounces) instant potato flakes

⅓ cup Carnation Nonfat Dry Milk Powder

1 teaspoon dried parsley flakes

¼ teaspoon black pepper

8 slices reduced-calorie white bread

Place roast beef in microwave and microwave on BAKE (60% power) for 2 minutes. Meanwhile, in a small saucepan, warm gravy. Also, in a medium saucepan, bring water to a boil. Remove water from heat. Stir in potato flakes, dry milk powder, parsley flakes, and black pepper. Mix well using a fork. For each serving, place 1 slice bread on plate, arrange ¼ of the roast beef slices over the bread, and top with another slice of bread; cut in half, spoon about ½ cup mashed potatoes in center of each sandwich and spoon about ⅓ cup gravy over top.

Each serving equals:

HE: 2 Bread • 1 Protein • ¼ Skim Milk • ¼ Slider • 18 Optional Calories

221 Calories • 1 gm Fat • 19 gm Protein • 34 gm Carbohydrate • 976 mg Sodium • 1 gm Fiber

DIABETIC: 2½ Starch • 1 Meat

Quick BBQ Beef Sandwiches

● Serves 4 (½ cup filling)

½ cup finely diced green bell pepper

½ cup finely chopped onion

1 (10¾ ounce) can Healthy Request Tomato Soup

1 tablespoon Brown Sugar Twin

1 tablespoon white vinegar

1 teaspoon Worcestershire sauce

1 (6-ounce) package Healthy Choice sliced 97% fat-free roast beef, shredded

4 reduced-calorie hamburger buns

In a large skillet sprayed with butter-flavored cooking spray, sauté green pepper and onion for 5 minutes or until tender. Stir in tomato soup, Brown Sugar Twin, vinegar, and Worcestershire sauce. Bring mixture to a boil. Add roast beef. Mix well to combine. Lower heat and simmer for 10 minutes, stirring occasionally. Serve on hamburger buns.

Each serving equals:

HE: 1 Protein • 1 Bread • ½ Vegetable • ½ Slider •
6 Optional Calories

187 Calories • 3 gm Fat • 11 gm Protein • 29 gm Carbohydrate •
817 mg Sodium • 4 gm Fiber

DIABETIC: 2 Starch • 1 Meat

Sea Breeze Tuna Macaroni Salad

This colorful tuna and macaroni salad is as fresh and cool as the wind off the ocean in late afternoon! I don't know about you, but I can always use new ways to serve tuna fish—it's a great source of protein, and you can often buy lots on sale.

☻ Serves 4 (1 cup)

> 2 cups cold cooked shell macaroni, rinsed and drained
> 1 (6-ounce) can white tuna, packed in water, drained and flaked
> 1 cup chopped fresh tomato
> ¾ cup chopped unpeeled cucumber
> ¼ cup (1 ounce) sliced ripe olives
> ¼ cup chopped onion
> ⅓ cup Kraft Fat Free Italian Dressing
> 2 tablespoons Kraft fat-free mayonnaise

In a large bowl, combine macaroni, tuna, tomato, cucumber, olives, and onion. Add Italian dressing and mayonnaise. Mix gently to combine. Cover and refrigerate for at least 15 minutes. Gently stir again just before serving.

HINT: 1⅓ cups uncooked shell macaroni usually cooks to about 2 cups.

Each serving equals:

HE: 1 Vegetable • 1 Bread • ¾ Protein • ¼ Fat • 16 Optional Calories

---

182 Calories • 2 gm Fat • 15 gm Protein • 26 gm Carbohydrate • 450 mg Sodium • 27 mg Calcium • 2 gm Fiber

---

DIABETIC: 2 Vegetable • 1½ Meat • 1 Starch

Easy Cheesy Tuna and Noodles

Instead of a classic baked tuna casserole, try stirring up this skillet version when it's too hot to turn on the oven! It's luscious, it's creamy—and it's good for you, too!   ☻   Serves 4 (1 full cup)

2 cups hot cooked noodles, rinsed and drained

1 (6-ounce) can white tuna, packed in water, rinsed and drained

½ cup (one 2.5-ounce jar) sliced mushrooms, undrained

2 cups (one 16-ounce can) cut green beans, rinsed and drained

1 (10¾-ounce) can Healthy Request Cream of Mushroom Soup

1 teaspoon dried onion flakes

1 teaspoon dried parsley flakes

⅛ teaspoon black pepper

¾ cup (3 ounces) shredded Kraft reduced-fat Cheddar cheese

In a large skillet, combine noodles, tuna, undrained mushrooms, and green beans. Add mushroom soup, onion flakes, parsley flakes, and black pepper. Mix well to combine. Cook over medium heat for 10 minutes, or until mixture is heated through, stirring occasionally. Stir in Cheddar cheese. Lower heat and simmer for 5 minutes or until cheese melts, stirring often.

HINT: 1¾ cups uncooked noodles usually cooks to about 2 cups.

Each serving equals:

HE: 1¾ Protein • 1¼ Vegetable • 1 Bread • ½ Slider •
1 Optional Calorie

266 Calories • 6 gm Fat • 22 gm Protein • 31 gm Carbohydrate •
712 mg Sodium • 224 mg Calcium • 2 gm Fiber

DIABETIC: 2 Meat • 1½ Starch • 1 Vegetable

Baked Parmesan Fish Fillets

Even if you've been baking fish for years, give this method a try—and see if you don't hear cheers from all around the table! You'll find that beneath a crusty top, your fish is wonderfully soft and flaky (not at all dried out as sometimes happens).

❤ Serves 4

> 16 ounces white fish, cut into 4 pieces
> ¼ cup skim milk
> ¼ cup Kraft fat-free mayonnaise
> ¼ cup (¾ ounce) grated Kraft fat-free Parmesan cheese
> 1 teaspoon dried parsley flakes
> 1 teaspoon chili seasoning
> ¼ teaspoon black pepper

Preheat oven to 350 degrees. Spray an 8-by-8-inch baking dish with butter-flavored cooking spray. Dip fish pieces into skim milk. Place fish in prepared baking dish. In a small bowl, combine mayonnaise, Parmesan cheese, parsley flakes, chili seasoning, black pepper, and any remaining skim milk. Evenly spread mixture over top of fish pieces. Cover and bake for 15 minutes. Uncover and continue baking for 10 minutes, or until fish flakes easily. Divide into 4 servings.

Each serving equals:

HE: 1¾ Protein • 16 Optional Calories

133 Calories • 1 gm Fat • 23 gm Protein • 8 gm Carbohydrate • 343 mg Sodium • 64 mg Calcium • 1 gm Fiber

DIABETIC: 3½ Meat • ½ Starch/Carbohydrate

Mex-Italian Chicken Pita

Have you noticed that even the fast-food chains have added pita sandwiches to their menus? They've only now learned what we've known for a while—stuffing a tasty filling into one of these Middle Eastern breads is a great way to deliver lots of flavorful goodness in one handy package!   ☻   Serves 4

1 full cup (6 ounces) diced cooked chicken breast
½ cup finely diced celery
½ cup chunky salsa (mild, medium, or hot)
⅓ cup Kraft fat-free mayonnaise
1 teaspoon dried parsley flakes
2 pita rounds, halved
½ cup finely shredded lettuce
2 tablespoons Kraft Fat Free Italian Dressing

In a medium bowl, combine chicken and celery. Add salsa, mayonnaise, and parsley flakes. Mix well to combine. Spoon about ½ cup chicken mixture into each pita half. In a small bowl, combine lettuce and Italian dressing. Mix gently to coat lettuce. Sprinkle about 2 tablespoons lettuce mixture over top of each pita sandwich. Serve at once or cover and refrigerate until ready to serve.

HINTS: 1. If you don't have leftovers, purchase a chunk of cooked chicken breast from your local deli.
   2. To make opening pita rounds easier, place pita halves on a paper towel and microwave on HIGH for 10 seconds. Remove and gently press open.

Each serving equals:

HE: 1½ Protein • 1 Bread • ¾ Vegetable • 17 Optional Calories

174 Calories • 2 gm Fat • 16 gm Protein • 23 gm Carbohydrate • 566 mg Sodium • 81 mg Calcium • 1 gm Fiber

DIABETIC: 1½ Meat • 1 Starch • 1 Vegetable

South Seas Chicken Salad

Okay, I admit it—Cliff and I haven't yet been to the South Seas, at least not for real! But with dishes like this, we've definitely visited there in our minds, and in our mouths. Why not let this taste of the tropics be your passport to a wonderful culinary vacation tonight?   ☻   Serves 4 (¾ cup)

> 1½ cups (8 ounces) diced cooked chicken breast
> 1 cup (6 ounces) sliced Thompson grapes
> 1 cup (one 11-ounce can) mandarin oranges, rinsed and drained
> ¼ cup Kraft Fat Free Ranch Dressing
> 2 tablespoons Kraft fat-free mayonnaise
> 1 tablespoon + 1 teaspoon flaked coconut
> ¼ cup (1 ounce) chopped walnuts

In a medium bowl, combine chicken, grapes, and mandarin oranges. Add Ranch dressing, mayonnaise, coconut, and walnuts. Mix well to combine. Cover and refrigerate for at least 20 minutes. Gently stir again just before serving.

HINT: If you don't have leftovers, purchase a chunk of cooked chicken breast from your local deli.

Each serving equals:

HE: 2¼ Protein • 1 Fruit • ½ Fat • ¼ Slider • 10 Optional Calories

223 Calories • 7 gm Fat • 19 gm Protein • 21 gm Carbohydrate • 211 mg Sodium • 27 mg Calcium • 1 gm Fiber

DIABETIC: 2 Meat • 1 Fruit • 1 Fat • ½ Starch/Carbohydrate

Gringo Chicken Stew

This is the busy mom's favorite kind of cooking—combine half the ingredients and simmer, then add a few more, and simmer till it's done! Isn't it great to stir up a stew with old-fashioned flavor that doesn't take hours to prepare?

● Serves 4 (1½ cups)

> 2 cups (one 16-ounce can) Healthy Request Chicken Broth
> 1 full cup (6 ounces) diced cooked chicken breast
> ½ cup chopped onion
> ¾ cup chopped celery
> 1 cup (5 ounces) diced raw potatoes
> 1 cup frozen whole-kernel corn, thawed
> 1 cup frozen sliced carrots, thawed
> ½ teaspoon dried minced garlic
> ¼ teaspoon black pepper
> 1¾ cups (one 15-ounce can) Hunt's Chunky Tomato Sauce
> ¾ cup chunky salsa (mild, medium, or hot)
> 1 teaspoon dried parsley flakes

In a large saucepan, combine chicken broth, chicken, onion, celery, potatoes, corn, carrots, garlic, and black pepper. Bring mixture to a boil. Lower heat, cover, and simmer for 15 minutes. Add tomato sauce, salsa, and parsley flakes. Mix well to combine. Continue simmering for 5 minutes, stirring occasionally.

HINTS: 1. If you don't have leftovers, purchase a chunk of cooked chicken breast from your local deli.
2. Thaw corn and carrots by placing in a colander and rinsing under hot water for one minute.

Each serving equals:

HE: 3¼ Vegetable • 1½ Protein • ¾ Bread • 8 Optional Calories

194 Calories • 2 gm Fat • 18 gm Protein • 26 gm Carbohydrate • 970 mg Sodium • 92 mg Calcium • 4 gm Fiber

DIABETIC: 3 Vegetable • 1½ Meat • 1 Starch

Grilled Chicken with Italian Vegetables

Instead of grilling with oil or butter, dipping your poultry in fat-free dressing is a terrific way to add lots of flavor. Topping it with a skillet sauté of fresh veggies will please the eye as well as the palate! ◑ Serves 4

16 ounces skinned and boned uncooked chicken breasts, cut into 4 pieces
¾ cup Kraft Fat Free Italian Dressing
1¼ cups chopped unpeeled zucchini
½ cup chopped onion
1 cup chopped fresh mushrooms
1¼ cups chopped fresh tomatoes
¼ cup (1 ounce) sliced ripe olives
1 teaspoon Italian seasoning
¼ teaspoon dried minced garlic
1 tablespoon fresh parsley or 1 teaspoon dried parsley flakes

Dip chicken pieces in Italian dressing. In a large skillet sprayed with olive oil–flavored cooking spray, brown chicken pieces about 4 minutes on each side. Meanwhile, pour any remaining Italian dressing into another large skillet sprayed with olive oil–flavored cooking spray. Add zucchini, onion, mushrooms, tomatoes, olives, Italian seasoning, garlic, and parsley flakes. Mix well to combine. Cook over medium heat until chicken is tender, stirring occasionally. When serving, spoon full ½ cup vegetable mixture over each piece of chicken.

Each serving equals:

HE: 3 Protein • 2 Vegetable • ¼ Fat • ¼ Slider • 4 Optional Calories

178 Calories • 2 gm Fat • 28 gm Protein • 12 gm Carbohydrate • 620 mg Sodium • 35 mg Calcium • 2 gm Fiber

DIABETIC: 3 Meat • 2 Vegetable • ½ Fat

French Parmesan Chicken Mélange

Speedy and scrumptious—isn't that the perfect "formula" for dining success at your house? There's something so old-timey and warm-spirited about a creamy chicken and noodles dish, I bet even your busy kids and distracted husband will linger a bit longer at the table.   ❤   Serves 4 (1 full cup)

1 full cup (6 ounces) diced cooked chicken breast

½ cup frozen peas, thawed

½ cup (one 2.5-ounce jar) sliced mushrooms, drained

¼ cup (one 2-ounce jar) chopped pimiento, drained

2 cups hot cooked noodles, rinsed and drained

1 (10¾-ounce) can Healthy Request Cream of Chicken Soup

¼ cup Kraft Fat Free French Dressing

1 teaspoon dried parsley flakes

⅛ teaspoon black pepper

¼ cup (¾ ounce) grated Kraft fat-free Parmesan cheese

In a large skillet sprayed with butter-flavored cooking spray, sauté chicken for 3 to 4 minutes. Stir in peas, mushrooms, pimiento, and noodles. Add chicken soup, French dressing, parsley flakes, and black pepper. Mix well to combine. Stir in Parmesan cheese. Lower heat and simmer for 5 minutes, or until mixture is heated through, stirring often.

HINTS: 1. If you don't have leftovers, purchase a chunk of cooked chicken breast from your local deli.
2. Thaw peas by placing in a colander and rinsing under hot water for one minute.
3. 1¾ cups uncooked noodles usually cooks to about 2 cups.

Each serving equals:

HE: 1¾ Protein • 1¼ Bread • ¼ Vegetable • ¾ Slider • 10 Optional Calories

280 Calories • 4 gm Fat • 21 gm Protein • 40 gm Carbohydrate • 653 mg Sodium • 25 mg Calcium • 4 gm Fiber

DIABETIC: 2½ Starch/Carbohydrate • 2 Meat

Terrific Taco Toss

I decided to create a healthy version of this restaurant mainstay that doesn't sacrifice one bit of great taste. With all this crunch and fresh flavor, I bet you won't miss all that extra fat!   ☻   Serves 4 (2 cups)

  8 ounces ground 90% lean turkey or beef
  4 cups finely shredded lettuce
  1¼ cups diced fresh tomatoes
  ¼ cup chopped onion
  ¼ cup (1 ounce) sliced ripe olives
  ⅔ cup (2¼ ounces) shredded Kraft reduced-fat Cheddar cheese
  ½ cup (1½ ounces) crushed Doritos Reduced Fat Nacho Chips
  ⅓ cup Kraft Fat Free Catalina or French Dressing
  2 tablespoons taco seasoning
  ¼ cup Land O Lakes no-fat sour cream

In a large skillet sprayed with olive oil–flavored cooking spray, brown meat. Place skillet on a wire rack and let set 5 minutes. Meanwhile, in a large bowl, combine lettuce, tomatoes, onion, olives, and Cheddar cheese. Stir in slightly cooled meat and crushed nacho chips. Add Catalina dressing and taco seasoning. Mix gently to combine. When serving, top each with 1 tablespoon sour cream.

Each serving equals:

HE: 3 Vegetable • 2¼ Protein • ½ Bread • ¼ Fat • ½ Slider • 8 Optional Calories

217 Calories • 9 gm Fat • 16 gm Protein • 18 gm Carbohydrate • 564 mg Sodium • 142 mg Calcium • 2 gm Fiber

DIABETIC: 2 Meat • 1 Starch/Carbohydrate • ½ Vegetable

Acapulco Golden Burgers

Instead of topping burgers with cheese and a spicy sauce, I decided to mix them right into the meat—making each bite a delectable surprise! Even if you can't make it to the Mexican Riviera this week (or even this year!), you can dine like a world traveler with this tangy variation. ❂ Serves 6

16 ounces ground 90% lean turkey or beef

6 tablespoons (1½ ounces) dried fine bread crumbs

¾ cup chunky salsa (mild, medium, or hot)☆

1 teaspoon chili seasoning

1 teaspoon dried parsley flakes

⅓ cup (1½ ounces) shredded Kraft reduced-fat Cheddar cheese

6 reduced-calorie hamburger buns

3 tablespoons Land O Lakes no-fat sour cream

In a large bowl, combine meat, bread crumbs, ¼ cup salsa, chili seasoning, parsley flakes, and Cheddar cheese. Using a ⅓ cup measuring cup as a guide, form into 6 patties. Place patties in a large skillet sprayed with olive oil–flavored cooking spray and brown about 4 to 5 minutes on each side or to desired degree of doneness. For each serving, place a patty between a bun and top with 1 tablespoon salsa and ½ tablespoon sour cream.

Each serving equals:

HE: 2⅓ Protein • 1⅓ Bread • ¼ Vegetable • 8 Optional Calories

237 Calories • 9 gm Fat • 18 gm Protein • 21 gm Carbohydrate • 462 mg Sodium • 109 mg Calcium • 1 gm Fiber

DIABETIC: 2 Meat • 1½ Starch • ½ Vegetable

Easy Italian Meat Loaf

If you haven't ever made a meat loaf in the microwave, this is a great one to try. By blending the veggies right into the meat, then letting those magic waves do their stuff, you'll end up with a scrumptious and satisfying dinner festive enough to be served in Venice! ☻ Serves 6

16 ounces ground 90% lean turkey or beef

½ cup (one 2.5-ounce jar) sliced mushrooms, drained

¼ cup chopped onion

¼ cup chopped green bell pepper

6 tablespoons (1½ ounces) dried fine bread crumbs

1 teaspoon Italian seasoning

¼ teaspoon dried minced garlic

1¾ cups (one 15-ounce can) Hunt's Chunky Tomato Sauce☆

2 teaspoons Sugar Twin or Sprinkle Sweet

1 teaspoon dried parsley flakes

In a large bowl, combine meat, mushrooms, onion, green pepper, bread crumbs, Italian seasoning, garlic, and ¼ cup tomato sauce. Mix well to combine. Place a small custard cup in center of a deep-dish 9-inch glass pie plate or use a microwave ring mold. Evenly spread meat mixture into pie plate. In a small bowl, combine remaining 1½ cups tomato sauce, Sugar Twin, and parsley flakes. Spread sauce mixture evenly over meat. Microwave on HIGH (100% power) for 10 minutes. Turn dish and continue microwaving on HIGH an additional 8 minutes. Place pie plate on a wire rack and let set for 5 minutes. Cut into 6 servings.

Each serving equals:

HE: 2 Protein • 1½ Vegetable • ⅓ Bread • 1 Optional Calorie

154 Calories • 6 gm Fat • 15 gm Protein • 10 gm Carbohydrate • 648 mg Sodium • 19 mg Calcium • 2 gm Fiber

DIABETIC: 2 Meat • 2 Vegetable *or* 2 Meat • ½ Starch/Carbohydrate

Chow Mein Meat Loaf

Every country-style restaurant boasts a meat loaf recipe "like Mom used to make," but what if you'd like to try a new approach to this all-American classic? Stirring some crunchy noodles and a taste of the Far East into this family favorite is fun and flavorful!   ☻   Serves 6

> *16 ounces ground 90% lean turkey or beef*
> *¾ cup finely chopped onion*
> *1 (1 ⅛-ounce) package Kikkoman Chow Mein Seasoning Mix*
> *¼ teaspoon black pepper*
> *¼ cup water*
> *1 cup (2¼ ounces) coarsely crushed chow mein noodles*

In a large bowl, combine meat, onion, seasoning mix, black pepper, and water. Add chow mein noodles. Mix well to combine. Place a small custard cup in center of a deep-dish 9-inch glass pie plate or use microwave ring mold. Evenly spread meat mixture into plate. Microwave on HIGH (100% power) for 10 minutes. Turn dish and continue microwaving on HIGH for an additional 6 minutes. Place pie plate on a wire rack and let set for 5 minutes. Cut into 6 servings.

Each serving equals:

HE: 2 Protein • ½ Bread • ¼ Vegetable • 16 Optional Calories

164 Calories • 8 gm Fat • 15 gm Protein • 8 gm Carbohydrate • 580 mg Sodium • 5 mg Calcium • 0 gm Fiber

DIABETIC: 2 Meat • ½ Starch

Spanish Rice Skillet

Here's another of my quick-and-thrifty main dish delights that make supper so easy to fix. When you start with the right ingredients, you can't help but succeed! Olé! ☻ Serves 4 (1 cup)

> *8 ounces ground 90% lean turkey or beef*
> *¼ cup chopped onion*
> *1¾ cups (one 15-ounce can) stewed tomatoes, undrained*
> *½ cup water*
> *½ cup frozen whole-kernel corn, thawed*
> *2 teaspoons chili seasoning*
> *1 tablespoon Brown Sugar Twin*
> *1 cup (3 ounces) uncooked Minute Rice*

In a large skillet sprayed with olive oil–flavored cooking spray, brown meat and onion. Add undrained stewed tomatoes, water, corn, chili seasoning, and Brown Sugar Twin. Mix well to combine. Bring mixture to a boil. Stir in uncooked rice. Cover, remove from heat, and let set for 5 minutes. Fluff with a fork before serving.

HINT: Thaw corn by placing in a colander and rinsing under hot water for one minute.

Each serving equals:

HE: 1½ Protein • 1 Vegetable • 1 Bread • 1 Optional Calorie

173 Calories • 5 gm Fat • 12 gm Protein • 20 mg Carbohydrate • 416 mg Sodium • 67 mg Calcium • 2 gm Fiber

DIABETIC: 1½ Meat • 1 Vegetable • 1 Starch

Cabbage Lover's Meat Dish

This recipe was inspired by all those wonderful cabbage-and-meat dishes that come to us from the old traditions of Eastern Europe. It provides both great flavor and wonderful texture. ☻ Serves 6 (1 full cup)

16 ounces ground 90% lean turkey or beef

1 cup chopped onion

4 cups shredded cabbage

¼ teaspoon black pepper

1 (10¾-ounce) can Healthy Request Tomato Soup

1 cup Healthy Request Tomato Juice or any reduced-sodium tomato juice

2 teaspoons chili seasoning

1 tablespoon Brown Sugar Twin

1 cup (3 ounces) uncooked Minute Rice

In a large skillet sprayed with butter-flavored cooking spray, brown meat and onion. Stir in cabbage and black pepper. Continue cooking for 8 to 10 minutes, or until cabbage is just tender, stirring often. Add tomato soup, tomato juice, chili seasoning, and Brown Sugar Twin. Mix well to combine. Bring mixture to a boil. Stir in uncooked rice. Cover, remove from heat, and let set for 5 minutes. Fluff with a fork before serving.

HINT: 4 cups purchased coleslaw mix may be used in place of cabbage.

Each serving equals:

HE: 2 Protein • 2 Vegetable • ½ Bread • ¼ Slider •
11 Optional Calories

191 Calories • 7 gm Fat • 15 gm Protein • 17 gm Carbohydrate •
257 mg Sodium • 35 mg Calcium • 2 gm Fiber

DIABETIC: 2 Meat • 1 Vegetable • 1 Starch

Taco-Time Pie

I've always loved the ease of prepared rolls as the basis for an easy entree, and this recipe provides a super-simple and satisfying Tex-Mex main dish! As you bring it to the table, you'll hear shouts of joy all around you!   ☻   Serves 8

1 (8-ounce) can Pillsbury Reduced Fat Crescent Rolls

8 ounces ground 90% lean turkey or beef

1¾ cups (one 15-ounce can) Hunt's Chunky Tomato Sauce

1 cup chunky salsa (mild, medium, or hot)

1 tablespoon taco seasoning

¾ cup (3 ounces) shredded Kraft reduced-fat Cheddar cheese

½ cup (2 ounces) sliced ripe olives

1 cup finely shredded lettuce

½ cup chopped fresh tomato

Preheat oven to 375 degrees. Spray a 12-inch pizza pan with olive oil–flavored cooking spray. Separate rolls into 8 triangles. Place triangles on prepared pan and make a crust being sure to seal perforations. Prick bottom and sides with the tines of a fork. Bake for 8 to 10 minutes or until golden brown. Meanwhile, in a large skillet sprayed with olive oil–flavored cooking spray, brown meat. Stir in tomato sauce, salsa, and taco seasoning. Simmer for 5 minutes. Spread meat sauce mixture evenly over baked crust. Sprinkle Cheddar cheese evenly over top. Continue baking for 5 minutes or until cheese melts. Place pizza pan on a wire rack and let set for 5 minutes. Top with olives, lettuce, and tomato. Cut into 8 wedges.

HINT: Good served with no-fat sour cream, but don't forget to count the few additional calories.

Each serving equals:

HE: 1½ Vegetable • 1¼ Protein • 1 Bread • ¼ Fat

215 Calories • 9 gm Fat • 11 gm Protein • 20 gm Carbohydrate • 883 mg Sodium • 86 mg Calcium • 1 gm Fiber

DIABETIC: 1½ Vegetable • 1 Meat • 1 Starch • ½ Fat

Mexican Potluck

I'm a big fan of using a glass 8-cup measure to stir up most of my pie recipes, but you'll find that it's also the perfect "pot" for microwave dinners. This tasty meal-in-minutes blends the flavors of this popular cuisine in a true culinary "treaty"!

❂ Serves 4 (1 full cup)

 8 ounces ground 90% lean turkey or beef
 1¾ cups (3 ounces) uncooked noodles
 ½ cup chopped onion
 ½ cup chopped green bell pepper
 ¼ teaspoon dried minced garlic
 1 cup chunky salsa (mild, medium, or hot)
 1¾ cups (one 15-ounce can) Hunt's Chunky Tomato Sauce
 1 teaspoon chili seasoning
 ½ cup (one 2.5-ounce jar) sliced mushrooms, drained
 ¼ cup (1 ounce) sliced ripe olives
 ⅓ cup (1½ ounces) shredded Kraft reduced-fat Cheddar cheese
 ¼ cup (¾ ounce) grated Kraft fat-free Parmesan cheese

Place meat in a plastic colander and set colander in a 9-inch glass pie plate. Microwave on HIGH (100% power) for 4 minutes or until meat is browned, stirring after 2 minutes. In an 8-cup glass measuring bowl, combine meat, uncooked noodles, onion, green pepper, garlic, salsa, and tomato sauce. Add chili seasoning, mushrooms, and olives. Mix well to combine. Cover and continue microwaving on HIGH for 10 minutes, stirring after 5 minutes. Evenly sprinkle Cheddar cheese over top. Re-cover and continue microwaving on HIGH for 2 minutes or until cheese melts. Let set for 5 minutes. When serving, sprinkle 1 tablespoon Parmesan cheese over each serving.

Each serving equals:

HE: 3 Vegetable • 2¼ Protein • 1 Bread • ¼ Fat

280 Calories • 8 gm Fat • 18 gm Protein • 34 gm Carbohydrate • 1334 mg Sodium • 171 mg Calcium • 5 gm Fiber

DIABETIC: 3½ Vegetable • 2½ Meat • 1 Starch • ½ Fat

Easy Pork Chop Suey

Here's a cooking trick you might not know: Slicing your veggies (like the celery in this recipe) on a slant instead of straight across provides a wider "canvas" for the sauce you're cooking with to "join hands" with that ingredient and intensify the taste! ☻ Serves 4

2 cups thin bias-cut celery slices

½ cup chopped onion

½ cup chopped green bell pepper

2 tablespoons cornstarch

1 tablespoon reduced-sodium soy sauce

2 cups (one 16-ounce can) Healthy Request Chicken Broth

1 cup (one 8-ounce can) sliced water chestnuts, rinsed and drained

2 cups (10 ounces) diced lean cooked pork

2 cups hot cooked rice

In a large skillet sprayed with butter-flavored cooking spray, sauté celery, onion, and green pepper for 5 minutes or just until tender. In a small bowl, combine cornstarch, soy sauce, and chicken broth. Stir cornstarch mixture into vegetable mixture. Add water chestnuts and pork. Mix well to combine. Continue cooking until mixture thickens, stirring often. For each serving, place ½ cup rice on a plate and spoon about 1 full cup pork mixture over top.

HINTS: 1. If you don't have leftovers, purchase a chunk of lean cooked pork roast from your local deli.

2. 1⅓ cups uncooked rice usually cooks to about 2 cups.

Each serving equals:

HE: 2½ Protein • 1½ Vegetable • 1½ Bread • 8 Optional Calories

265 Calories • 5 gm Fat • 23 gm Protein • 32 gm Carbohydrate • 521 mg Sodium • 58 mg Calcium • 3 gm Fiber

DIABETIC: 3 Meat • 1½ Starch • 1 Vegetable

Grande Pork Casserole

Roast pork is so full of flavor, a little goes a long way. That's why, when you add only ten ounces of meat to this short list of ingredients, you can actually serve six!

○ Serves 6 (1 cup)

2 cups (10 ounces) diced cooked lean roast pork
1 cup (3 ounces) uncooked Minute Rice
1¾ cups (one 14½-ounce can) stewed tomatoes, coarsely chopped and undrained
¼ cup chopped onion
1½ cups frozen corn, thawed
1½ teaspoons chili seasoning
¼ teaspoon black pepper

Place roast pork in an 8-cup glass measuring bowl. Add uncooked rice, undrained stewed tomatoes, onion, corn, chili seasoning, and black pepper. Mix well to combine. Cover and microwave on HIGH (100% power) for 13 to 15 minutes, stirring after every 5 minutes. Let set for 2 to 3 minutes before serving.

HINTS: 1. If you don't have leftovers, purchase a chunk of cooked lean roast pork from your local deli.
2. Thaw corn by placing in a colander and rinsing under hot water for one minute.

Each serving equals:

HE: 1⅔ Protein • 1 Bread • ⅔ Vegetable

146 Calories • 2 gm Fat • 13 gm Protein • 19 gm Carbohydrate • 244 mg Sodium • 51 mg Calcium • 2 gm Fiber

DIABETIC: 1½ Meat • 1 Starch • ½ Vegetable

Easy Ham and Cabbage

This tasty new version of an old-fashioned favorite cooks up fast—but it sure doesn't taste like you hurried to "slap" it on the table! Use your favorite mustard to give it a little zing, and be careful not to overcook the cabbage. You want tender, not limp. ☻ Serves 4 (1¼ cups)

> 1½ cups (9 ounces) finely chopped Dubuque 97% fat-free ham or any extra-lean
>   ham
> 4 cups shredded cabbage
> ⅓ cup (1 ounce) uncooked Minute Rice
> ½ cup chopped onion
> 1¾ cups (one 15-ounce can) Hunt's Chunky Tomato Sauce
> 2 teaspoons prepared mustard
> 1 tablespoon Brown Sugar Twin
> ¼ teaspoon black pepper

In an 8-cup glass measuring bowl, combine ham, cabbage, uncooked rice, and onion. Add tomato sauce, mustard, Brown Sugar Twin, and black pepper. Mix well to combine. Cover and microwave on HIGH (100% power) for 12 to 15 minutes or until cabbage and rice are tender, stirring after 6 minutes.

HINT: Purchased coleslaw mix may be used in place of cabbage.

Each serving equals:

HE: 4 Vegetable • 1½ Protein • ¼ Bread

126 Calories • 2 gm Fat • 12 gm Protein • 15 gm Carbohydrate • 1201 mg Sodium • 41 mg Calcium • 4 gm Fiber

DIABETIC: 2 Vegetable • 1½ Meat • ½ Starch

Hawaiian Bean Hash

Instead of serving pork and beans straight from the can (how dull!), why not add a few tasty ingredients to make it sparkle like a hula dancer's eyes as she tosses a fragrant lei around your neck and says welcome? It's enough to warm up even the coldest midwinter night.   ☽   Serves 6 (1 cup)

> 20 ounces (two 16-ounce cans) navy beans, rinsed and drained
> 1 cup (one 8-ounce can) Hunt's Tomato Sauce
> 1½ cups (9 ounces) diced Dubuque 97% fat-free ham or any extra-lean ham
> 1 cup (one 8-ounce can) pineapple chunks, packed in fruit juice, drained
> 1 tablespoon dried onion flakes
> 2 teaspoons prepared mustard
> 2 tablespoons Brown Sugar Twin

In a large skillet sprayed with butter-flavored cooking spray, combine navy beans, tomato sauce, ham, and pineapple. Stir in onion flakes, mustard, and Brown Sugar Twin. Bring mixture to a boil. Lower heat and simmer for 15 minutes, stirring occasionally.

Each serving equals:

HE: 2⅔ Protein • ⅓ Fruit • 2 Optional Calories

222 Calories • 2 gm Fat • 16 gm Protein • 35 gm Carbohydrate • 674 mg Sodium • 83 mg Calcium • 9 gm Fiber

DIABETIC: 2 Meat • 1 Starch • ½ Fruit

Polynesian Ham Medley

Okay, so you don't have the space or the inclination to throw a luau featuring a whole roast pig! (I don't either!) But here's a fun way to enjoy that delicious island treat without leaving home. � Serves 4

1½ cups (9 ounces) diced Dubuque 97% fat-free ham or any extra-lean ham

1 cup (one 8-ounce can) pineapple tidbits, packed in fruit juice, undrained

1 cup coarsely chopped green bell pepper

1 tablespoon cornstarch

2 tablespoons Brown Sugar Twin

2 tablespoons white vinegar

1 tablespoon reduced-sodium soy sauce

½ cup water

2 cups hot cooked rice

In a large skillet sprayed with butter-flavored cooking spray, brown ham. Add undrained pineapple and green pepper. Mix well to combine. Lower heat, cover and simmer for 10 minutes, stirring occasionally. In a small bowl, combine cornstarch and Brown Sugar Twin. Stir in vinegar, soy sauce, and water. Add cornstarch mixture to ham mixture. Mix well to combine. Continue cooking until sauce thickens and mixture starts to boil, stirring often. For each serving, place ½ cup hot rice on a plate and spoon a full ½ cup ham mixture over top.

HINTS: 1. If you can't find pineapple tidbits, use chunk pineapple and coarsely chop.
2. 1⅓ cups uncooked rice usually cooks to about 2 cups.

Each serving equals:

HE: 1½ Protein • 1 Bread • ½ Fruit • ½ Vegetable • 3 Optional Calories

198 Calories • 2 gm Fat • 12 gm Protein • 33 gm Carbohydrate • 609 mg Sodium • 18 mg Calcium • 1 gm Fiber

DIABETIC: 1½ Meat • 1½ Starch • ½ Fruit

Mexicali Franks and Potatoes

Here's a quick and speedy sauté filled with all your kids' favorites—hash browns, frankfurters, and corn! When you need some fresh ideas for a skillet supper, this one should top the list.   ☻   Serves 4 (1 cup)

3 cups (10 ounces) shredded loose-packed frozen potatoes
½ cup chopped onion
½ cup chopped green bell pepper
8 ounces Healthy Choice 97% fat-free frankfurters, sliced
1 cup (one 8-ounce can) whole-kernel corn, rinsed and drained
⅛ teaspoon black pepper
1 teaspoon chili seasoning

In a large skillet sprayed with butter-flavored cooking spray, sauté potatoes, onion, and green pepper for 5 minutes or until almost tender. Stir in frankfurters. Continue to cook over medium heat until frankfurters begin to brown. Add corn, black pepper, and chili seasoning. Mix well to combine. Lower heat and simmer for 10 minutes, or until mixture is heated through, stirring occasionally.

HINT: Mr. Dell's frozen shredded potatoes are a good choice, or raw shredded potatoes may be used in place of frozen potatoes.

Each serving equals:

HE: 1⅓ Protein • 1 Bread • ½ Vegetable

161 Calories • 1 gm Fat • 11 gm Protein • 27 gm Carbohydrate •
578 mg Sodium • 12 mg Calcium • 3 gm Fiber

DIABETIC: 2 Starch • 1 Meat

Creole Frankfurters

Even when the radio's playing "Baby, It's Cold Outside," you can warm up the chilliest day with a dish that celebrates the spicy cuisine of the Old South! You won't even have to call the family to dinner, because this dish smells as delightful as it tastes!   ☻   Serves 4 (1 cup)

> 8 ounces Healthy Choice 97% fat-free frankfurters, sliced
> 1/2 cup chopped green bell pepper
> 1/2 cup chopped onion
> 1¾ cups (one 15-ounce can) Hunt's Chunky Tomato Sauce
> 1/2 cup frozen corn, thawed
> 1 teaspoon chili seasoning
> 1 tablespoon Brown Sugar Twin
> 1½ cups hot cooked rotini pasta, rinsed and drained

In a large skillet sprayed with butter-flavored cooking spray, sauté frankfurters, green pepper, and onion for 5 minutes. Stir in tomato sauce, corn, chili seasoning, and Brown Sugar Twin. Add rotini pasta. Mix well to combine. Lower heat and simmer for 10 minutes, or until mixture is heated through, stirring occasionally.

HINTS: 1. Thaw corn by placing in a colander and rinsing under hot water for one minute.
         2. 1 cup uncooked rotini pasta usually cooks to about 1½ cups.

Each serving equals:

HE: 2¼ Vegetable • 1⅓ Protein • 1 Bread • 1 Optional Calorie

185 Calories • 1 gm Fat • 12 gm Protein • 32 gm Carbohydrate •
1277 mg Sodium • 9 mg Calcium • 3 gm Fiber

DIABETIC: 2 Vegetable • 1½ Starch • 1 Meat

Desserts

Just like the old ad campaign—"Did she or didn't she?"—everyone will wonder if you made these luscious desserts from scratch, especially when they know you had no time to do it! It takes just a few minutes to whip up my Bonanza Banana Butterscotch Pie or create a real dazzler with Caribbean Pineapple Cheesecake, so when anyone asks what bakery produced such gorgeous creations, just smile mysteriously and murmur, "It's a secret."

Hot Spiced Fruit Sundae

Instead of choosing a high-calorie sundae topping, why not spoon this fruity blend over ice cream or frozen yogurt instead? It's pretty, it tastes great, and because it's served warm, it feels like a special treat instead of a "diet" dish!

☻ Serves 4

2 cups (two 8-ounce cans) fruit cocktail, packed in fruit juice, undrained
½ teaspoon apple pie spice
2 cups Wells' Blue Bunny sugar- and fat-free vanilla ice cream

In a small saucepan, combine undrained fruit cocktail and apple pie spice. Cook over medium heat for 5 minutes or until mixture is heated through. For each sundae, place ½ cup ice cream in a dessert dish and spoon ½ cup warm fruit mixture over top. Serve at once.

HINT: If you can't find Wells' Blue Bunny ice cream, use any sugar- and fat-free ice cream.

Each serving equals:

HE: 1 Fruit • ¾ Slider

144 Calories • 0 gm Fat • 4 gm Protein • 32 mg Carbohydrate • 55 mg Sodium • 130 mg Calcium • 1 gm Fiber

DIABETIC: 1 Fruit • 1 Starch/Carbohydrate

Peach Banana Ambrosia

Instead of just peeling and eating a banana, or opening a can of peaches and spooning them out, why not blend the two with just enough coconut to make it a heavenly day? ☻ Serves 4

2 cups (2 medium) sliced bananas
2 cups (one 16-ounce can) sliced peaches, packed in fruit juice, drained, and ¼
    cup liquid reserved
¼ cup Cool Whip Lite
1 tablespoon + 1 teaspoon flaked coconut

Place ½ cup bananas into 4 dessert dishes. Evenly arrange peaches over top. Drizzle 1 tablespoon reserved peach juice over each dish. Top each with 1 tablespoon Cool Whip Lite and garnish with 1 teaspoon coconut. Refrigerate for at least 15 minutes.

HINT: To prevent bananas from turning brown, mix with 1 teaspoon lemon juice or sprinkle with Fruit Fresh.

Each serving equals:

HE: 2 Fruit • 5 Optional Calories

145 Calories • 1 gm Fat • 1 gm Protein • 33 gm Carbohydrate •
0 mg Sodium • 12 mg Calcium • 3 gm Fiber

DIABETIC: 2 Fruit

Creamy Eggnog Pudding

Even if Christmas is months away, why wait to enjoy this special flavor treat? If you're feeling festive, serve this dessert in your most attractive goblets—and you might think it's New Year's Eve! ☺ Serves 4

1 (4-serving) package JELL-O sugar-free instant vanilla pudding mix
2 cups skim milk
½ cup Cool Whip Free
1 teaspoon brandy extract
¼ teaspoon ground nutmeg

In a medium bowl, combine dry pudding mix and skim milk. Mix well using a wire whisk. Blend in Cool Whip Free and brandy extract. Spoon pudding mixture into 4 dessert dishes. Sprinkle nutmeg over top. Refrigerate for at least 20 minutes.

Each serving equals:

HE: ½ Skim Milk • ½ Slider

76 Calories • 0 gm Fat • 4 gm Protein • 15 gm Carbohydrate • 393 mg Sodium • 151 mg Calcium • 0 gm Fiber

DIABETIC: ½ Skim Milk •
½ Starch/Carbohydrate *or* 1 Starch/Carbohydrate

Crème Maple Dessert

The dessert that inspired this recipe, crème caramel, is very high in sugar and fat, but I was determined to find a way to deliver that sweet and creamy flavor in a healthy way. Try this, and see if you agree that I succeeded in my quest!

♥ Serves 4

1 (4-serving) package JELL-O sugar-free instant vanilla pudding mix
2 cups skim milk
2 tablespoons Cary's Sugar Free Maple Syrup☆
¼ cup Cool Whip Lite

In a medium bowl, combine dry pudding mix and skim milk. Mix well using a wire whisk. Pour 1 teaspoon maple syrup into 4 dessert dishes. Evenly spoon pudding mixture into dishes. Refrigerate for at least 15 minutes. When serving, garnish each with 1 tablespoon Cool Whip Lite and drizzle ½ teaspoon maple syrup over top.

Each serving equals:

HE: ½ Skim Milk • ¼ Slider • 10 Optional Calories

72 Calories • 0 gm Fat • 4 gm Protein • 14 gm Carbohydrate • 410 mg Sodium • 151 mg Calcium • 0 gm Fiber

DIABETIC: ½ Skim Milk •
½ Starch/Carbohydrate *or* 1 Starch/Carbohydrate

Cupid's Pudding Delight

If you want to show the one you love just how much you treasure his or her affection, this is the perfectly pretty dessert to serve! Smooth and creamy, lush and fruity, it's my idea of "love-on-a-spoon!" ☻ Serves 4

2¼ cups frozen unsweetened raspberries, thawed and drained
Sugar substitute to equal 1 tablespoon sugar
1 (4-serving) package JELL-O sugar-free instant chocolate fudge pudding mix
1 cup skim milk
¾ cup Yoplait plain fat-free yogurt
4 tablespoons Cool Whip Lite

In a small bowl, combine raspberries and sugar substitute. Reserve ¼ cup for garnish. Evenly spoon half of remaining berries into 4 dessert dishes. In a medium bowl, combine dry pudding mix, skim milk, and yogurt. Mix well using a wire whisk. Spoon half of pudding mixture evenly over raspberries. Evenly top each with remaining raspberries and remaining pudding. Refrigerate for at least 15 minutes. When serving, top each with 1 tablespoon Cool Whip Lite and garnish with 1 tablespoon of reserved raspberry mixture.

Each serving equals:

HE: ¾ Fruit • ½ Skim Milk • ½ Slider • 7 Optional Calories

121 Calories • 1 gm Fat • 6 gm Protein • 22 gm Carbohydrate •
394 mg Sodium • 174 mg Calcium • 3 gm Fiber

DIABETIC: 1½ Starch/Carbohydrate

Butterscotch Graham Cracker Parfait

Simple and fun, this easy pudding parfait looks pretty enough to serve at a party! I used regular graham crackers in this recipe, but you might want to try it sometime with the cinnamon or chocolate ones—just for a bit of a change.

○ Serves 4

1 (4-serving) package JELL-O sugar-free instant butterscotch pudding mix
2 cups skim milk
8 tablespoons purchased graham cracker crumbs or 9 (2½-inch) graham cracker squares, made into crumbs☆
¼ cup Cool Whip Lite
2 maraschino cherries, halved

In a medium bowl, combine dry pudding mix and skim milk. Mix well using a wire whisk. Spoon ¼ cup pudding mixture into 4 parfait dishes. Sprinkle 2 tablespoons graham cracker crumbs over top of each. Layer ¼ cup pudding mixture over crumbs. Top each with 1 tablespoon Cool Whip Lite and garnish with maraschino cherry half. Refrigerate for at least 15 minutes.

HINT: A self-seal sandwich bag works great for crushing graham crackers.

Each serving equals:

HE: ¾ Bread • ½ Skim Milk • ¼ Slider • 10 Optional Calories

109 Calories • 1 gm Fat • 5 gm Protein • 20 gm Carbohydrate • 454 mg Sodium • 151 mg Calcium • 0 gm Fiber

DIABETIC: 1 Starch/Carbohydrate • ½ Skim Milk

Chocolate Cherry Pudding

Who among us doesn't love surprises when it comes to dessert? When I was creating this recipe, I decided what would please me most when I spooned up the first bite—pecans! The flavor combination of chocolate and cherry is always festive, so it'll be no surprise when everyone asks "How soon can we have this again?" ☻ Serves 8

> 2 (4-serving) packages JELL-O sugar-free instant chocolate pudding mix
> 1 (4-serving) package JELL-O sugar-free cherry gelatin
> 1⅓ cups Carnation Nonfat Dry Milk Powder
> 3 cups water
> 1 cup Cool Whip Free☆
> ¼ cup (1 ounce) chopped pecans
> 4 teaspoons Hershey's Lite Chocolate Syrup
> 4 maraschino cherries, halved

In a large bowl, combine dry pudding mixes, dry gelatin, dry milk powder, and water. Mix well using a wire whisk. Stir in ½ cup Cool Whip Free and pecans. Spoon mixture into 8 dessert dishes. Refrigerate for at least 15 minutes. When serving, top each with 1 tablespoon Cool Whip Free, drizzle ½ teaspoon chocolate syrup over top, and garnish with a maraschino cherry half.

Each serving equals:

HE: ½ Skim Milk • ½ Fat • ¾ Slider

111 Calories • 3 gm Fat • 5 gm Protein • 16 gm Carbohydrate • 257 mg Sodium • 141 mg Calcium • 0 gm Fiber

DIABETIC: 1 Starch/Carbohydrate • ½ Skim Milk • ½ Fat

Coconut Pistachio Parfait

There's something almost magical about a layered dessert. Maybe it's because it seems to promise an abundance of flavors in one tall glass. This parfait brims over with taste and texture, coolness and color. No one will blame you if you put on a party hat to serve this one!   ❂   Serves 6

1 (4-serving) package JELL-O sugar-free instant pistachio pudding mix

⅓ cup Carnation Nonfat Dry Milk Powder

¾ cup Yoplait plain fat-free yogurt

1 cup (one 8-ounce can) crushed pineapple, packed in fruit juice, undrained

½ cup water

1 teaspoon coconut extract

¾ cup Cool Whip Free

1 cup (one 11-ounce can) mandarin oranges, rinsed and drained

½ cup (1 ounce) miniature marshmallows

1 tablespoon flaked coconut

In a medium bowl, combine dry pudding mix and dry milk powder. Add yogurt, undrained pineapple, and water. Mix well using a wire whisk. Blend in coconut extract and Cool Whip Free. Add mandarin oranges and marshmallows. Mix gently to combine. Spoon mixture evenly into 6 parfait or dessert dishes. Evenly sprinkle ½ teaspoon coconut over top of each. Refrigerate for at least 15 minutes.

Each serving equals:

HE: ⅔ Fruit • ⅓ Skim Milk • ½ Slider

116 Calories • 0 gm Fat • 3 gm Protein • 26 gm Carbohydrate •
264 mg Sodium • 113 mg Calcium • 0 gm Fiber

DIABETIC: 1 Starch/Carbohydrate • ½ Fruit

Easy Vanilla Fruit Parfait

Uh-oh, the doorbell rang and unexpected guests appeared. What can you serve in a hurry that doesn't look like you "threw" it together? I vote for this creamy parfait easily stirred up from ingredients you're likely to have in the house.

❤ Serves 6

1 (4-serving) package JELL-O sugar-free instant vanilla pudding mix

⅓ cup Carnation Nonfat Dry Milk Powder

¾ cup Yoplait plain fat-free yogurt

2 cups (one 16-ounce can) fruit cocktail, packed in fruit juice, undrained

1 cup (1 medium) diced banana

6 tablespoons Cool Whip Lite

3 maraschino cherries, halved

In a medium bowl, combine dry pudding mix, dry milk powder, yogurt, and undrained fruit cocktail. Mix well using a wire whisk. Spoon mixture into 6 parfait or dessert dishes. Top each with 1 tablespoon Cool Whip Lite and garnish with a maraschino cherry half.

HINT: To prevent banana from turning brown, mix with 1 teaspoon lemon juice or sprinkle with Fruit Fresh.

Each serving equals:

HE: 1 Fruit • ⅓ Skim Milk • ¼ Slider • 12 Optional Calories

116 Calories • 0 gm Fat • 4 gm Protein • 25 gm Carbohydrate • 259 mg Sodium • 111 mg Calcium • 1 gm Fiber

DIABETIC: 1 Fruit • ½ Starch

Hawaiian Sunset Rice Pudding

There's something so delightfully cozy about rice pudding, isn't there? For me, it brings back wonderful memories of childhood. But because variety makes life interesting, I've blended in the sweet flavors of Hawaii to tempt your taste buds just as a tropical sunset dazzles your eyes! ☻ Serves 4

¾ cup Yoplait plain fat-free yogurt
½ cup Cool Whip Free
Sugar substitute to equal 2 tablespoons sugar
2 cups (two 8-ounce cans) crushed pineapple, packed in fruit juice, drained, and 1
*   tablespoon liquid reserved*
½ teaspoon vanilla extract
2 cups cold cooked rice
4 teaspoons flaked coconut

In a medium bowl, combine yogurt, Cool Whip Free, sugar substitute, reserved pineapple juice, and vanilla extract. Add rice, pineapple, and coconut. Mix well to combine. Evenly spoon mixture into 4 dessert dishes. Refrigerate for at least 15 minutes.

HINTS: 1. 1⅓ cups uncooked rice usually cooks to about 2 cups.
          2. Good topped with 1 tablespoon Cool Whip Lite, but don't forget to count the few additional calories.

Each serving equals:

HE: 1 Fruit • 1 Bread • ¼ Skim Milk • ¼ Slider •
3 Optional Calories

196 Calories • 0 gm Fat • 5 gm Protein • 44 gm Carbohydrate •
42 mg Sodium • 109 mg Calcium • 1 gm Fiber

DIABETIC: 1½ Starch/Carbohydrate • 1 Fruit

Layered Fruit Dessert

Try arranging graham crackers in the bottom of your cake pan for a quick "home-made" piecrust—it's an easy and healthy first layer for any dessert! This colorful and fruity blend is a perfect finale for your next barbecue.   ♥   Serves 6

12 (2½-inch) graham cracker squares

1 cup (1 medium) sliced banana

2 cups sliced fresh strawberries

1 (4-serving) package JELL-O sugar-free instant vanilla pudding mix

⅔ cup Carnation Nonfat Dry Milk Powder

1 cup (one 8-ounce can) crushed pineapple, packed in fruit juice, undrained

¾ cup water

¾ cup Cool Whip Free

1 teaspoon coconut extract

2 tablespoons flaked coconut

Arrange graham crackers in bottom of a 9-by-9-inch cake pan. Evenly layer banana and strawberries over crackers. In a large bowl, combine dry pudding mix, dry milk powder, undrained pineapple, and water. Mix well using a wire whisk. Evenly spoon pudding mixture over fruit. Refrigerate for at least 20 minutes. Cut into 6 servings. In a small bowl, combine Cool Whip Free and coconut extract. When serving, top each piece with a full tablespoon of topping mixture and garnish with 1 teaspoon coconut.

HINT: To prevent banana from turning brown, mix with 1 teaspoon lemon juice or sprinkle with Fruit Fresh.

Each serving equals:

HE: 1 Fruit • ⅔ Bread • ⅓ Skim Milk • ¼ Slider •
16 Optional Calories

166 Calories • 2 gm Fat • 4 gm Protein • 33 gm Carbohydrate •
316 mg Sodium • 106 mg Calcium • 2 gm Fiber

DIABETIC: 1 Fruit • 1 Starch/Carbohydrate • ½ Skim Milk

Applesauce Cream Pie

One of my favorite tricks when creating recipes is to layer the flavors. You can see how I do it in this one, as I blend apple juice, applesauce, apple pie spice, and apple butter to produce a luscious dessert that dazzles!   ☻   Serves 8

1 (4-serving) package JELL-O sugar-free instant vanilla pudding mix

⅔ cup Carnation Nonfat Dry Milk Powder

1 cup unsweetened apple juice

1 cup unsweetened applesauce

½ teaspoon apple pie spice

1 (6-ounce) Keebler graham cracker piecrust

2 tablespoons apple butter

¾ cup Cool Whip Free

In a large bowl, combine dry pudding mix and dry milk powder. Add apple juice, applesauce, and apple pie spice. Mix well using a wire whisk. Evenly spread mixture into piecrust. Refrigerate for at least 1 hour. Cut into 8 servings. Just before serving, in a small bowl, combine apple butter and Cool Whip Free. Evenly garnish each piece with 2 tablespoons topping mixture.

Each serving equals:

HE: ½ Fruit • ½ Bread • ¾ Slider • 19 Optional Calories

161 Calories • 5 gm Fat • 3 gm Protein • 33 gm Carbohydrate • 303 mg Sodium • 72 mg Calcium • 1 gm Fiber

DIABETIC: 1 Starch/Carbohydrate • 1 Fat • ½ Fruit

Butterscotch Coconut-Cream Pie

Give this unusual combo of flavors a chance, and you'll be so glad you did! I think coconut is a festive ingredient all by itself, and when blended with this luscious, creamy filling, produces a dessert worthy of applause! ☻ Serves 8

1 (4-serving) package JELL-O sugar-free instant butterscotch pudding mix
⅓ cup Carnation Nonfat Dry Milk Powder
¾ cup Yoplait plain fat-free yogurt
1 cup water
1 cup Cool Whip Free☆
1 teaspoon coconut extract
3 tablespoons flaked coconut☆
1 (6-ounce) Keebler graham cracker piecrust

In a large bowl, combine dry pudding mix, dry milk powder, yogurt, and water. Mix well using a wire whisk. Blend in ¼ cup Cool Whip Free, coconut extract, and 2 tablespoons coconut. Evenly spread mixture into piecrust. Refrigerate for at least 10 minutes. Spread remaining ¾ cup Cool Whip Free evenly over set filling. Sprinkle remaining 1 tablespoon coconut over top. Cut into 8 servings.

Each serving equals:

HE: ½ Bread • ¼ Skim Milk • 1 Slider • 4 Optional Calories

166 Calories • 6 gm Fat • 3 gm Protein • 25 gm Carbohydrate • 345 mg Sodium • 80 mg Calcium • 1 gm Fiber

DIABETIC: 1½ Starch/Carbohydrate • ½ Fat

Bonanza Banana Butterscotch Pie

If you're like my daughter, Becky, you love butterscotch and bananas! This is the ideal dessert for fans of "B" and "B"—a speedy special delivery that tells your family how much you care. ☻ Serves 8

> 2 cups (2 medium) sliced bananas
> 1 (6-ounce) Keebler shortbread piecrust
> 1 (4-serving) package JELL-O sugar-free instant banana pudding mix
> 1⅓ cups Carnation Nonfat Dry Milk Powder☆
> 2¼ cups water☆
> 1 (4-serving) package JELL-O sugar-free instant butterscotch pudding mix
> ½ cup Cool Whip Free
> 2 tablespoons (½ ounce) chopped pecans

Evenly arrange bananas in piecrust. In a large bowl, combine dry banana pudding mix, ⅔ cup dry milk powder, and 1¼ cups water. Mix well using a wire whisk. Pour pudding mixture evenly over bananas. Refrigerate while preparing topping. In the same bowl, combine dry butterscotch pudding mix, remaining ⅔ cup dry milk powder, and remaining 1 cup water. Mix well using a wire whisk. Blend in Cool Whip Free. Spread topping mixture evenly over banana layer. Sprinkle pecans evenly over top. Refrigerate for at least 15 minutes. Cut into 8 servings.

Each serving equals:

> HE: ½ Fruit • ½ Skim Milk • ½ Bread • ¼ Fat • 1 Slider •
> 3 Optional Calories
> _____
> 213 Calories • 5 gm Fat • 5 gm Protein • 37 gm Carbohydrate •
> 540 mg Sodium • 141 mg Calcium • 1 gm Fiber
> _____
> DIABETIC: 2 Starch/Carbohydrate • ½ Fruit • ½ Fat

Banana Cream Pie with Chocolate Frosting

Here's a scrumptious dessert that looks and tastes deliciously home baked but takes very little time to prepare. The frosting is so rich and creamy, you'll have lots of volunteers to lick the bowl!   ☻   Serves 8

> 2 cups (2 medium) sliced bananas
> 1 (6-ounce) Keebler chocolate piecrust
> 1 (4-serving) package JELL-O sugar-free instant banana pudding mix
> ⅔ cup Carnation Nonfat Dry Milk Powder
> 1½ cups water
> 1 cup Cool Whip Free☆
> 2 teaspoons vanilla extract☆
> 2 tablespoons unsweetened cocoa
> 2 tablespoons Sugar Twin or Sprinkle Sweet
> 2 (2½-inch) chocolate graham cracker squares, made into fine crumbs

Evenly arrange bananas in piecrust. In a large bowl, combine dry pudding mix, dry milk powder, and water. Mix well using a wire whisk. Stir in ¼ cup Cool Whip Free and 1 teaspoon vanilla extract. Pour pudding mixture evenly over bananas. Refrigerate while preparing topping. In a small bowl, combine remaining ¾ cup Cool Whip Free, cocoa, Sugar Twin, and remaining 1 teaspoon vanilla extract. Spread mixture evenly over set filling. Evenly sprinkle crumbs over top. Refrigerate for at least 15 minutes. Cut into 8 servings.

HINT: To prevent bananas from turning brown, mix with 1 teaspoon lemon juice or sprinkle with Fruit Fresh.

Each serving equals:

HE: ½ Bread • ½ Fruit • ¼ Skim Milk • 1 Slider •
9 Optional Calories

193 Calories • 5 gm Fat • 4 gm Protein • 34 gm Carbohydrate •
320 mg Sodium • 76 mg Calcium • 2 gm Fiber

DIABETIC: 1½ Starch/Carbohydrate • 1 Fat • ½ Fruit

Pistachio Chocolate Chip Cream Pie

Here's a colorful and creamy finale that will cheer chocolate fans and please those lovers of the nut called pistachio! If you'd like to try a little cook's trick I learned, drizzle the syrup in a few circles on top of your pie, then alternately draw a knife blade from the center to the outer rim, or the rim to the center—and you'll get a pretty design! ● Serves 8

1 (4-serving) package JELL-O sugar-free instant pistachio pudding mix

⅓ cup Carnation Nonfat Dry Milk Powder

¾ cup Yoplait plain fat-free yogurt

¾ cup water

3 tablespoons (¾ ounce) mini milk chocolate chips

1 cup Cool Whip Free☆

1 (6-ounce) Keebler chocolate piecrust

2 teaspoons Hershey's Lite Chocolate Syrup

In a medium bowl, combine dry pudding mix and dry milk powder. Add yogurt and water. Mix well using a wire whisk. Blend in chocolate chips and ¼ cup Cool Whip Free. Evenly spread mixture into piecrust. Refrigerate for at least 15 minutes. Just before serving, spread remaining ¾ cup Cool Whip Free over set filling and drizzle chocolate syrup over top. Cut into 8 servings.

Each serving equals:

HE: ½ Bread • ¼ Skim Milk • ¾ Slider • 19 Optional Calories

174 Calories • 6 gm Fat • 3 gm Protein • 27 gm Carbohydrate • 298 mg Sodium • 78 mg Calcium • 1 gm Fiber

DIABETIC: 1½ Starch/Carbohydrate • 1 Fat

Aloha Chocolate Cream Pie

As smooth as a hula dancer's graceful gestures, this flavorful pie is a delectable meal's end certain to delight your family and friends. If pineapple is one of your favorite pleasures, this pie is for you.　　❂　　Serves 8

> 1 (4-serving) package JELL-O sugar-free instant chocolate pudding mix
> ⅔ cup Carnation Nonfat Dry Milk Powder
> 2 cups (two 8-ounce cans) crushed pineapple, packed in fruit juice, undrained
> ½ cup Cool Whip Free
> 1 teaspoon coconut extract
> 1 (6-ounce) Keebler chocolate piecrust
> 2 tablespoons flaked coconut

In a large bowl, combine dry pudding mix and dry milk powder. Add undrained pineapple. Mix well using a wire whisk. Blend in Cool Whip Free and coconut extract. Evenly spread mixture into piecrust. Sprinkle coconut evenly over top. Refrigerate for at least 20 minutes. Cut into 8 servings.

HINT: Good topped with 1 tablespoon Cool Whip Lite, but don't forget to count the few additional calories.

Each serving equals:

HE: ½ Fruit • ½ Bread • ¼ Skim Milk • ¾ Slider • 16 Optional Calories

193 Calories • 5 gm Fat • 4 gm Protein • 33 gm Carbohydrate • 302 mg Sodium • 78 mg Calcium • 1 gm Fiber

DIABETIC: 1½ Starch/Carbohydrate • ½ Fruit • ½ Fat

Chocolate Cookies and Cream Pie

This classic ice cream flavor is beloved by so many, and now it's the heart of a healthy pie! Freezing the pie intensifies the flavors, but don't forget to allow time for it to thaw when you're ready to serve it. ☻ Serves 8

1 (4-serving) package JELL-O sugar-free instant white chocolate pudding mix
⅓ cup Carnation Nonfat Dry Milk Powder
½ cup water
¾ cup Yoplait plain fat-free yogurt
1 cup Cool Whip Free
8 (2½-inch) chocolate graham cracker squares☆
1 (6-ounce) Keebler chocolate piecrust

In a medium bowl, combine dry pudding mix, dry milk powder, water, and yogurt. Mix well using a wire whisk. Blend in Cool Whip Free. Break 6 graham crackers into bite-size pieces. Blend into pudding mixture. Spread mixture into piecrust. Crush remaining 2 graham crackers into fine crumbs. Evenly sprinkle crumbs over top. Refrigerate for at least 30 minutes. Cut into 8 servings.

HINTS:　1. A self-seal sandwich bag works great for crushing graham crackers.
　　　　 2. Can also be frozen and served partially frozen for an "ice cream" feel.

Each serving equals:

HE: ⅔ Bread • ¼ Skim Milk • 1 Slider • 3 Optional Calories

173 Calories • 5 gm Fat • 4 gm Protein • 28 gm Carbohydrate • 324 mg Sodium • 77 mg Calcium • 1 gm Fiber

DIABETIC: 1½ Starch/Carbohydrate • ½ Fat

Turtle Pie

♥ Serves 8

1 (4-serving) package JELL-O sugar-free instant chocolate pudding mix

⅔ cup Carnation Nonfat Dry Milk Powder

1¼ cups water

¾ cup Cool Whip Lite☆

¼ cup (1 ounce) chopped pecans☆

1 (6-ounce) Keebler graham cracker piecrust

1 tablespoon (¼ ounce) mini chocolate chips

1 tablespoon caramel sauce

In a large bowl, combine dry pudding mix, dry milk powder, and water. Mix well using a wire whisk. Blend in ¼ cup Cool Whip Lite. Stir in 2 tablespoons pecans. Spread mixture evenly into piecrust. Evenly spread remaining ½ cup Cool Whip Lite over pudding mixture. Sprinkle chocolate chips and remaining 2 tablespoons pecans over top. Refrigerate for at least 20 minutes. Just before serving, drizzle caramel sauce over top. Cut into 8 servings.

Each serving equals:

HE: ½ Bread • ½ Fat • ¼ Skim Milk • 1 Slider •
8 Optional Calories

---

188 Calories • 8 gm Fat • 4 gm Protein • 25 gm Carbohydrate •
340 mg Sodium • 1 gm Fiber

DIABETIC: 1½ Starch *or* Carbohydrate • 1 Fat

Caribbean Pineapple Cheesecake

I remember tasting something like this rich treat when Cliff and I enjoyed a cruise through the islands a few years ago. Even if the closest you'll get to the tropics this year is in your imagination, here's my gift to your tummy by way of Jamaica—a delectable dessert not soon forgotten!   ☻   Serves 8

> 2 (8-ounce) packages Philadelphia fat-free cream cheese
> 1 (4-serving) package JELL-O sugar-free instant vanilla pudding mix
> 1 (4-serving) package JELL-O sugar-free lemon gelatin
> ⅔ cup Carnation Nonfat Dry Milk Powder
> 2 cups (two 8-ounce cans) crushed pineapple, packed in fruit juice, undrained
> 1 cup Cool Whip Free
> 1 teaspoon coconut extract
> 1 teaspoon rum extract
> 1 (6-ounce) Keebler shortbread piecrust
> 2 tablespoons flaked coconut

In a large bowl, stir cream cheese with a spoon until soft. Add dry pudding mix, dry gelatin, dry milk powder, and undrained pineapple. Mix well using a wire whisk. Stir in Cool Whip Free, coconut extract, and rum extract. Evenly spread mixture into piecrust. Sprinkle coconut evenly over top. Refrigerate for at least 30 minutes. Cut into 8 servings.

Each serving equals:

HE: 1 Protein • ½ Fruit • ½ Bread • ¼ Skim Milk • 1 Slider • 6 Optional Calories

---

241 Calories • 5 gm Fat • 12 gm Protein • 37 gm Carbohydrate • 666 mg Sodium • 78 gm Calcium • 1 gm Fiber

---

DIABETIC: 2 Starch/Carbohydrate • 1 Meat • 1 Fat • ½ Fruit *or* 2½ Starch/Carbohydrate • 1 Meat • 1 Fat

Chocolate Almond Raspberry Pie

This is a perfect case of a dessert that looks fancy but couldn't be simpler to prepare! I chose raspberry spreadable fruit to line the piecrust, but you might want to experiment with any favorite flavor of your choice!   ☻   Serves 8

½ cup raspberry spreadable fruit☆
1 (6-ounce) Keebler chocolate piecrust
1 (8-ounce) package Philadelphia fat-free cream cheese
1 (4-serving) package JELL-O sugar-free instant chocolate pudding mix
⅔ cup Carnation Nonfat Dry Milk Powder
1½ cups water
½ teaspoon almond extract
¾ cup Cool Whip Free
2 tablespoons (½ ounce) chopped almonds
1 tablespoon (¼ ounce) mini chocolate chips

Spread ¼ cup spreadable fruit in bottom of piecrust. In a medium bowl, stir cream cheese with a spoon until soft. Add dry pudding mix, dry milk powder, water, and almond extract. Mix well using a wire whisk. Evenly pour mixture over spreadable fruit. Refrigerate while making topping. In a small bowl, stir remaining ¼ cup spreadable fruit with a spoon until soft. Stir in Cool Whip Free. Evenly spread topping mixture over set filling. Sprinkle almonds and chocolate chips evenly over top. Refrigerate for at least 15 minutes. Cut into 8 servings.

HINT: Spreadable fruit spreads best at room temperature.

Each serving equals:

HE: 1 Fruit • ½ Bread • ½ Protein • ¼ Skim Milk • ¾ Slider •
15 Optional Calories

226 Calories • 6 gm Fat • 7 gm Protein • 36 gm Carbohydrate •
470 mg Sodium • 74 mg Calcium • 1 gm Fiber

DIABETIC: 1 Fruit • 1 Starch • ½ Meat • ½ Fat

Buried Peanut Butter Treasure Pie

This pie is almost like a sundae, it's got so many fantastic flavors piled up! Topped with peanuts and chocolate, it's a special-occasion treat you can enjoy anytime, although I know it will make a hit at your next family reunion!

● Serves 8

1 (8-ounce) package Philadelphia fat-free cream cheese

¼ cup chunky Peter Pan reduced-fat peanut butter

1 (4-serving) package JELL-O sugar-free instant vanilla pudding mix

1⅓ cups Carnation Nonfat Dry Milk Powder☆

2 cups water☆

1 (6-ounce) Keebler chocolate piecrust

1 (4-serving) package JELL-O sugar-free instant chocolate pudding mix

½ teaspoon vanilla extract

¾ cup Cool Whip Free

2 teaspoons Hershey's Lite Chocolate Syrup

2 tablespoons (½ ounce) chopped dry roasted peanuts

In a medium bowl, stir cream cheese and peanut butter with a spoon until soft. Add dry vanilla pudding mix, ⅔ cup dry milk powder, and 1 cup water. Mix well using a wire whisk. Evenly spread mixture into piecrust. In a medium bowl, combine dry chocolate pudding mix, remaining ⅔ cup dry milk powder, and remaining 1 cup water. Mix well using a wire whisk. Blend in vanilla extract. Spread mixture over peanut butter layer. Refrigerate for at least 15 minutes. Just before serving, evenly spread Cool Whip Free over set chocolate layer, drizzle chocolate syrup over top, and garnish with peanuts. Cut into 8 servings.

Each serving equals:

HE: 1½ Protein • ⅔ Fat • ½ Skim Milk • ½ Fat • 1 Slider • 10 Optional Calories

273 Calories • 9 gm Fat • 12 gm Protein • 36 gm Carbohydrate • 713 mg Sodium • 141 mg Calcium • 1 gm Fiber

DIABETIC: 2 Starch/Carbohydrate • 1 Meat • 1 Fat

Decadent Peanut Butter Cheesecake

My friend Barbara will always select chunky peanut butter if given a choice, while I'm more apt to opt for creamy, but both of us love peanut butter—and think that a cheesecake to celebrate it is a great idea! This recipe is so rich, it's hard to believe that it's also healthy—but I always deliver what I promise . . . and I promise you it is! ☻ Serves 8

> 2 (8-ounce) packages Philadelphia fat-free cream cheese
> 6 tablespoons chunky or creamy Peter Pan reduced-fat peanut butter
> 1 (4-serving) package JELL-O sugar-free instant vanilla pudding mix
> ⅔ cup Carnation Nonfat Dry Milk Powder
> 1 cup water
> ¼ cup Cool Whip Free
> 1 teaspoon vanilla extract
> 1 (6-ounce) Keebler chocolate piecrust
> 1 tablespoon Hershey's Lite Chocolate Syrup

In a large bowl, stir cream cheese with a spoon until soft. Blend in peanut butter. Add dry pudding mix, dry milk powder, and water. Mix well using a wire whisk. Blend in Cool Whip Free and vanilla extract. Evenly spread mixture into piecrust. Refrigerate for at least 15 minutes. Just before serving, drizzle chocolate syrup over top. Cut into 8 servings.

Each serving equals:

HE: 1¾ Protein • ¾ Fat • ½ Bread • ¼ Skim Milk • ¾ Slider • 9 Optional Calories

253 Calories • 9 gm Fat • 14 gm Protein • 29 gm Carbohydrate • 695 mg Sodium • 76 mg Calcium • 1 gm Fiber

DIABETIC: 2 Protein • 1½ Starch/Carbohydrate • 1½ Fat

Banana Lemon Cream Pie

● Serves 8

3 cups (3 medium) finely diced bananas
1 (6-ounce) Keebler shortbread piecrust
1 (4-serving) package JELL-O sugar-free instant vanilla pudding mix
1 (4-serving) package JELL-O sugar-free lemon gelatin
⅔ cup Carnation Nonfat Dry Milk Powder
1⅓ cups Diet Mountain Dew
1 cup Cool Whip Lite☆
2 tablespoons (½ ounce) chopped pecans

Layer bananas in bottom of piecrust. In a large bowl, combine dry pudding mix, dry gelatin, dry milk powder, and Diet Mountain Dew. Mix well using a wire whisk. Blend in ¼ cup Cool Whip Lite. Spread pudding mixture evenly over bananas. Refrigerate 5 minutes. Evenly spread remaining ¾ cup Cool Whip Lite over set filling. Sprinkle pecans evenly over top. Refrigerate for at least 15 minutes. Cut into 8 servings.

HINT: To prevent bananas from turning brown, mix with 1 teaspoon lemon juice or sprinkle with Fruit Fresh.

Each serving equals:

HE: ¾ Fruit • ½ Bread • ¼ Skim Milk • ¼ Fat • 1 Slider • 7 Optional Calories

227 Calories • 7 gm Fat • 4 gm Protein • 37 gm Carbohydrate • 324 mg Sodium • 2 gm Fiber

DIABETIC: 1½ Starch • 1 Fruit • 1 Fat

Chocolate Peppermint Pie

● Serves 8

1 (4-serving) package JELL-O sugar-free instant chocolate pudding mix

⅔ cup Carnation Nonfat Dry Milk Powder

1¼ cups water

1 cup Cool Whip Lite☆

1 (6-ounce) Keebler chocolate piecrust

¾ teaspoon mint extract

3 to 4 drops green food coloring

1 tablespoon (¼ ounce) mini chocolate chips

In a medium bowl, combine dry pudding mix, dry milk powder, and water. Mix well using a wire whisk. Blend in ¼ cup Cool Whip Lite. Spread mixture evenly into piecrust. Refrigerate while preparing topping. In a small bowl, combine remaining ¾ cup Cool Whip Lite, mint extract, and green food coloring. Spread topping mixture evenly over pudding mixture. Sprinkle chocolate chips evenly over top. Refrigerate for at least 20 minutes. Cut into 8 servings.

Each serving equals:

HE: ½ Bread • ¼ Skim Milk • 1 Slider • 10 Optional Calories

166 Calories • 6 gm Fat • 4 gm Protein • 24 gm Carbohydrate • 296 mg Sodium • 1 gm Fiber

DIABETIC: 1½ Starch *or* Carbohydrate • 1 Fat

Lemon Fruit Tarts

● Serves 6

1 (8-ounce) package Philadelphia fat-free cream cheese

1 (4-serving) package JELL-O sugar-free lemon gelatin

½ cup Cool Whip Lite

1 (6-single serve) package Keebler graham cracker crusts

6 tablespoons spreadable fruit spread (any flavor)

In a medium bowl, stir cream cheese with a spoon until soft. Add dry gelatin and Cool Whip Lite. Continue stirring until well blended. Evenly spread cream cheese mixture into graham cracker crusts. Spread 1 tablespoon spreadable fruit over top of each. Refrigerate for at least 15 minutes.

HINT: Spreadable fruit spreads best at room temperature.

Each serving equals:

HE: 1 Fruit • ⅔ Protein • ½ Bread • ¾ Slider •
10 Optional Calories

194 Calories • 6 gm Fat • 7 gm Protein • 28 gm Carbohydrate •
408 mg Sodium • 0 gm Fiber

DIABETIC: 1 Fruit • 1 Fat • 1 Starch

Banana Isle Pudding Desserts

● Serves 4

1 (4-serving) package JELL-O sugar-free instant banana pudding mix
⅔ cup Carnation Nonfat Dry Milk Powder
1 cup water
1 cup (one 8-ounce can) crushed pineapple, packed in fruit juice, undrained
1 cup (1 medium) diced banana
½ cup Cool Whip Lite☆
½ teaspoon apple pie spice

In a large bowl, combine dry pudding mix, dry milk powder, and water. Mix well using a wire whisk. Stir in undrained pineapple and banana. Add ¼ cup Cool Whip Lite and apple pie spice. Mix well to combine. Spoon mixture into 4 dessert dishes. Refrigerate for at least 20 minutes. When serving, top each with 1 tablespoon Cool Whip Lite.

HINT: To prevent banana from turning brown, mix with 1 teaspoon lemon juice or sprinkle with Fruit Fresh.

Each serving equals:

HE: 1 Fruit • ½ Skim Milk • ½ Slider • 5 Optional Calories

157 Calories • 1 gm Fat • 5 gm Protein • 32 gm Carbohydrate • 403 mg Sodium • 1 gm Fiber

DIABETIC: 1 Fruit • ½ Starch • ½ Skim Milk

Cherry-Chocolate Pudding Treats

○ Serves 4

1 (4-serving) package JELL-O sugar-free instant chocolate pudding mix
⅔ cup Carnation Nonfat Dry Milk Powder
1½ cups water
¼ cup black cherry spreadable fruit spread
¼ cup Cool Whip Lite
4 teaspoons (⅓ ounce) chopped walnuts

In a medium bowl, combine dry pudding mix, dry milk powder, and water. Mix well using a wire whisk. Evenly spoon mixture into four dessert dishes. Refrigerate while preparing topping. In a small bowl, combine spreadable fruit and Cool Whip Lite. Mix gently to combine. Spoon mixture evenly over top of pudding. Sprinkle 1 teaspoon walnuts evenly over top of each. Refrigerate for at least 15 minutes.

Each serving equals:

HE: 1 Fruit • ½ Skim Milk • ½ Slider • 12 Optional Calories

146 Calories • 2 gm Fat • 5 gm Protein • 27 gm Carbohydrate • 408 mg Sodium • 0 gm Fiber

DIABETIC: 1 Fruit • ½ Skim Milk • ½ Starch

Lemon Cloud Fruit Dessert

◐ Serves 4

1 (4-serving) package JELL-O sugar-free instant vanilla pudding mix

1 (4-serving) package JELL-O sugar-free lemon gelatin

⅔ cup Carnation Nonfat Dry Milk Powder

2 cups (one 16-ounce can) fruit cocktail, packed in fruit juice, drained, and ½
    cup liquid reserved

1 cup water

½ cup Cool Whip Lite

½ cup (1 ounce) miniature marshmallows

In a medium bowl, combine dry pudding mix, dry gelatin, and dry milk powder. Add reserved fruit cocktail liquid and water. Mix well using a wire whisk. Blend in Cool Whip Lite, drained fruit cocktail, and marshmallows. Evenly spoon mixture into 4 dessert dishes. Refrigerate for at least 15 minutes.

Each serving equals:

HE: 1 Fruit • ½ Skim Milk • ½ Slider • 15 Optional Calories

169 Calories • 1 gm Fat • 6 gm Protein • 34 gm Carbohydrate •
453 mg Sodium • 1 gm Fiber

DIABETIC: 1 Starch *or* Carbohydrate • 1 Fruit

Chocolate Strawberry Mud Pie

○ Serves 8

2 cups sliced fresh strawberries

1 (6-ounce) Keebler chocolate piecrust

1 (4-serving) package JELL-O sugar-free instant chocolate pudding mix

⅔ cup Carnation Nonfat Dry Milk Powder

1¼ cups water

¾ cup Cool Whip Lite☆

1 teaspoon almond extract☆

2 tablespoons (½ ounce) finely chopped slivered almonds

2 teaspoons chocolate syrup

Layer strawberries in bottom of piecrust. In a large bowl, combine dry pudding mix, dry milk powder and water. Mix well using a wire whisk. Blend in ¼ cup Cool Whip Lite and ½ teaspoon almond extract. Spread pudding mixture evenly over strawberries. Refrigerate while preparing topping. In a small bowl, gently combine remaining ½ cup Cool Whip Lite, remaining ½ teaspoon almond extract and almonds. Spread topping mixture evenly over set filling. Drizzle chocolate syrup evenly over the top. Refrigerate for at least 15 minutes. Cut into 8 servings.

Each serving equals:

HE: ½ Bread • ¼ Fruit • ¼ Skim Milk • ¼ Fat • 1 Slider • 6 Optional Calories

183 Calories • 7 gm Fat • 4 gm Protein • 26 gm Carbohydrate • 298 mg Sodium • 1 gm Fiber

DIABETIC: 2 Starch *or* Carbohydrate • 1 Fat

Raspberry Chocolate Parfait

♥ Serves 4

1 (4-serving) package JELL-O sugar-free instant chocolate pudding mix

⅓ cup Carnation Nonfat Dry Milk Powder

1½ cups Yoplait plain fat-free yogurt

½ cup water

½ teaspoon almond extract

6 tablespoons purchased graham cracker crumbs or six (2½ inch) squares made into crumbs☆

¾ cup fresh red raspberries

¼ cup Cool Whip Lite

In a medium bowl, combine dry pudding mix and dry milk powder. Add yogurt and water. Mix well using a wire whisk. Blend in almond extract. Spoon about ¼ cup pudding mixture into 4 parfait or dessert dishes. Sprinkle about 1 tablespoon graham cracker crumbs over top of each. Reserve 4 raspberries. Evenly divide remaining raspberries among the four dishes. Evenly spoon remaining chocolate pudding (about ¼ cup each) over raspberries. Top each with 1 table-spoon Cool Whip Lite. Sprinkle about 1½ teaspoons crumbs over top of each and garnish with 1 reserved raspberry. Refrigerate for at least 15 minutes.

HINT: Frozen unsweetened raspberries, thawed and drained, may be substituted for fresh.

Each serving equals:

HE: ¾ Skim Milk • ½ Bread • ¼ Fruit • ½ Slider

174 Calories • 2 gm Fat • 9 gm Protein • 30 gm Carbohydrate • 493 mg Sodium • 1 gm Fiber

DIABETIC: 1 Skim Milk • 1 Carbohydrate • ½ Fat

Graham Cracker Caribbean Dessert

Serves 8 (¾ cup)

1 (4-serving) package JELL-O sugar-free instant banana pudding mix

1 cup Carnation Nonfat Dry Milk Powder☆

1 cup (one 8-ounce can) crushed pineapple, packed in fruit juice, drained, and ¼ cup liquid reserved

1¼ cups water

¾ cup Yoplait plain fat-free yogurt

1 teaspoon coconut extract

Sugar substitute to equal 2 tablespoons sugar

¾ cup Cool Whip Lite

1 cup (one 11-ounce can) mandarin oranges, rinsed and drained

12 (2½ inch) graham crackers, broken into pieces

In a large bowl, combine dry pudding mix and ⅔ cup dry milk powder. Add reserved pineapple liquid and water to dry pudding mixture. Mix well using a wire whisk. In a small bowl, combine yogurt and remaining ⅓ cup dry milk powder. Stir in coconut extract, sugar substitute, and Cool Whip Lite. Add yogurt mixture to pudding mixture. Mix gently to combine. Fold in pineapple, mandarin oranges, and graham cracker pieces. Cover and refrigerate for at least 15 minutes. Gently stir again just before serving.

HINT: If not serving for at least 30 minutes, gently stir graham cracker crumbs in when serving.

Each serving equals:

HE: ½ Skim Milk • ½ Fruit • ½ Bread • ¼ Slider • 9 Optional Calories

146 Calories • 2 gm Fat • 5 gm Protein • 27 gm Carbohydrate • 318 mg Sodium • 0 gm Fiber

DIABETIC: 1 Starch • ½ Skim Milk • ½ Fruit *or* 2 Carbohydrate

Fruit Cocktail Parfait

⚫ Serves 6

⅓ cup Carnation Nonfat Dry Milk Powder

¾ cup Yoplait plain fat-free yogurt

1 (4-serving) package JELL-O sugar-free instant pistachio pudding mix

2 cups (one 16-ounce can) fruit cocktail, packed in fruit juice, undrained

1 cup (1 medium) diced banana

6 tablespoons Cool Whip Lite

In a medium bowl, combine dry milk powder and yogurt. Stir in dry pudding mix. Add undrained fruit cocktail and banana. Mix gently to combine. Evenly spoon mixture into 6 parfait or dessert dishes. Top each with 1 tablespoon Cool Whip Lite. Refrigerate for at least 15 minutes.

HINT: To prevent banana from turning brown, mix with 1 teaspoon lemon juice or sprinkle with Fruit Fresh.

Each serving equals:

HE: 1 Fruit • ⅓ Skim Milk • ¼ Slider • 7 Optional Calories

121 Calories • 1 gm Fat • 3 gm Protein • 25 gm Carbohydrate • 259 mg Sodium • 1 gm Fiber

DIABETIC: 1 Fruit • ½ Starch

Hawaiian Banana Raisin Pie

○ Serves 8

1 cup (1 medium) diced banana

1 (6-ounce) Keebler graham cracker piecrust

1 (4-serving) package JELL-O sugar-free instant banana pudding mix

⅔ cup Carnation Nonfat Dry Milk Powder

1 cup (one 8-ounce can) crushed pineapple, packed in fruit juice, drained, and ¼
   cup liquid reserved

¾ cup water

1 cup Cool Whip Lite☆

½ cup raisins

1 teaspoon coconut extract

2 tablespoons flaked coconut

Layer banana in bottom of piecrust. In a medium bowl, combine dry pudding mix and dry milk powder. Add reserved pineapple liquid and water. Mix well using a wire whisk. Blend in ¼ cup Cool Whip Lite, drained pineapple, and raisins. Spread mixture evenly over bananas. Refrigerate 5 minutes. Meanwhile, in a small bowl, combine remaining ¾ cup Cool Whip Lite and coconut extract. Spread mixture evenly over set filling. Evenly sprinkle coconut over top. Refrigerate for at least 15 minutes. Cut into 8 servings.

HINTS: 1. To prevent banana from turning brown, mix with 1 teaspoon lemon juice or sprinkle with Fruit Fresh.

2. To plump up raisins without "cooking," place in a glass measuring cup and microwave on HIGH for 20 seconds.

Each serving equals:

HE: 1 Fruit • ½ Bread • ¼ Skim Milk • 1 Slider •
6 Optional Calories

230 Calories • 6 gm Fat • 4 gm Protein • 40 gm Carbohydrate •
298 mg Sodium • 2 gm Fiber

DIABETIC: 1½ Starch *or* Carbohydrate • 1 Fruit • 1 Fat

Yogurt Fruit Tarts

● Serves 6

¾ cup Yoplait plain fat-free yogurt

⅓ cup Carnation Nonfat Dry Milk Powder

6 tablespoons apricot spreadable fruit spread

¾ cup Cool Whip Lite

¼ teaspoon almond extract

1 (6-single serve) package Keebler graham cracker crusts

In a medium bowl, combine yogurt and dry milk powder. Stir in spreadable fruit and Cool Whip Lite. Add almond extract. Mix gently to combine. Evenly spoon mixture into graham cracker crusts. Refrigerate for at least 20 minutes.

Each serving equals:

HE: 1 Fruit • ½ Bread • ⅓ Skim Milk • ¾ Slider •
10 Optional Calories

186 Calories • 6 gm Fat • 3 gm Protein • 30 gm Carbohydrate •
177 mg Sodium • 0 gm Fiber

DIABETIC: 1 Fruit • 1 Starch • 1 Fat

Caribbean Coconut Cheesecake

● Serves 8

2 (8-ounce) packages Philadelphia fat-free cream cheese
1 (4-serving) package JELL-O sugar-free instant vanilla pudding mix
⅔ cup Carnation Nonfat Dry Milk Powder
1 cup water
1½ teaspoons coconut extract☆
1 teaspoon rum extract
1 cup Cool Whip Lite☆
1 (6-ounce) Keebler graham cracker piecrust
2 tablespoons flaked coconut

In a medium bowl, stir cream cheese with a spoon until soft. Add dry pudding mix, dry milk powder, and water. Mix well using a wire whisk. Blend in 1 teaspoon coconut extract, rum extract, and ¼ cup Cool Whip Lite. Spread mixture evenly into piecrust. Refrigerate while preparing topping. In a small bowl, combine remaining ¾ cup Cool Whip Lite and remaining ½ teaspoon coconut extract. Spread mixture evenly over filling. Evenly sprinkle coconut over top. Refrigerate for at least 20 minutes. Cut into 8 servings.

Each serving equals:

HE: 1 Protein • ½ Bread • ¼ Skim Milk • 1 Slider •
6 Optional Calories

198 Calories • 6 gm Fat • 11 gm Protein • 25 gm Carbohydrate •
674 mg Sodium • 1 gm Fiber

DIABETIC: 1½ Carbohydrate • 1 Meat • ½ Fat

Chocolate Banana Sunset Pie

● Serves 8

2 cups (2 medium) diced bananas

1 (6-ounce) Keebler chocolate piecrust

1 (4-serving) package JELL-O sugar-free instant chocolate pudding mix

⅔ cup Carnation Nonfat Dry Milk Powder

1 cup (one 8-ounce can) crushed pineapple, packed in fruit juice, drained, and ¼
     cup liquid reserved

1 cup water

1 cup Cool Whip Lite☆

1 teaspoon coconut extract

2 tablespoons flaked coconut

1 tablespoon (¼ ounce) mini chocolate chips

Layer bananas in bottom of piecrust. In a large bowl, combine dry pudding mix and dry milk powder. Add reserved pineapple liquid and water. Mix well using a wire whisk. Blend in ¼ cup Cool Whip Lite. Spread pudding mixture evenly over bananas. Refrigerate while preparing topping. In a small bowl, combine remaining ¾ cup Cool Whip Lite, coconut extract, and drained pineapple. Spread topping mixture evenly over pudding mixture. Evenly sprinkle coconut and chocolate chips over top. Refrigerate for at least 20 minutes. Cut into 8 servings.

HINT: To prevent bananas from turning brown, mix with 1 teaspoon lemon juice
     or sprinkle with Fruit Fresh.

Each serving equals:

HE: ¾ Fruit • ½ Bread • ¼ Skim Milk • 1 Slider •
13 Optional Calories

231 Calories • 7 gm Fat • 4 gm Protein • 38 gm Carbohydrate •
300 mg Sodium • 2 gm Fiber

DIABETIC: 1½ Starch or Carbohydrate • 1 Fruit • 1 Fat

Summer Breeze Rice Pudding

● Serves 6

1 (4-serving) package JELL-O sugar-free instant banana pudding mix
2 cups skim milk
2 cups cold cooked rice
1 cup (1 medium) diced banana
1½ cups fresh raspberries
6 tablespoons Cool Whip Lite

In a medium bowl, combine dry pudding mix and skim milk. Mix well using a wire whisk. Add rice. Mix well to combine. Gently fold in banana and raspberries. Evenly spoon mixture into 6 dessert dishes. Top each with 1 tablespoon Cool Whip Lite. Refrigerate for at least 20 minutes.

HINTS: 1. To prevent banana from turning brown, mix with 1 teaspoon lemon juice or sprinkle with Fruit Fresh.
2. 1⅓ cups uncooked rice usually cooks to about 2 cups.

Each serving equals:

HE: ⅔ Bread • ⅔ Fruit • ⅓ Skim Milk • ¼ Slider •
7 Optional Calories

145 Calories • 1 gm Fat • 4 gm Protein • 30 gm Carbohydrate •
271 mg Sodium • 2 gm Fiber

DIABETIC: 1 Starch • 1 Fruit

Banana Boat Parfait

⏺ Serves 4

1 (4-serving) package JELL-O sugar-free chocolate cook-and-serve pudding mix
⅔ cup Carnation Nonfat Dry Milk Powder
1½ cups water
1 teaspoon vanilla extract
2 cups (2 medium) diced bananas
½ cup (1 ounce) miniature marshmallows
¼ cup (1 ounce) chopped walnuts

In a medium saucepan, combine dry pudding mix, dry milk powder, and water. Cook over medium heat, stirring constantly with a wire whisk, until mixture thickens and starts to boil. Remove from heat. Stir in vanilla extract. Place saucepan on a wire rack and allow to cool for 10 minutes, stirring again after 5 minutes. Add bananas, marshmallows, and walnuts. Mix gently to combine. Evenly spoon mixture into 4 dessert dishes. Refrigerate for at least 20 minutes.

HINT: To prevent bananas from turning brown, mix with 1 teaspoon lemon juice or sprinkle with Fruit Fresh.

Each serving equals:

HE: 1 Fruit • ½ Skim Milk • ½ Fat • ¼ Protein • ¼ Slider • 18 Optional Calories

217 Calories • 5 gm Fat • 7 gm Protein • 36 gm Carbohydrate • 176 mg Sodium • 2 gm Fiber

DIABETIC: 1 Fruit • 1 Fat • 1 Starch or 2 Carbohydrate • 1 Fat

Butter Pecan Layered Pie

● Serves 8

1 (4-serving) package JELL-O sugar-free instant butterscotch pudding mix

⅔ cup Carnation Nonfat Dry Milk Powder

1¼ cups water

¼ cup (1 ounce) chopped pecans☆

1 (6-ounce) Keebler graham cracker piecrust

1 (8-ounce) package Philadelphia fat-free cream cheese

Sugar substitute to equal 2 tablespoons sugar

¾ cup Cool Whip Lite

1 teaspoon vanilla extract

In a large bowl, combine dry pudding mix, dry milk powder, and water. Mix well using a wire whisk. Stir in 2 tablespoons pecans. Spread mixture evenly into piecrust. Refrigerate while preparing topping. In a medium bowl, stir cream cheese with a spoon until soft. Add sugar substitute, Cool Whip Lite, and vanilla extract. Mix gently to combine. Spread topping mixture evenly over pudding mixture. Evenly sprinkle remaining 2 tablespoons pecans over top. Refrigerate for at least 20 minutes. Cut into 8 servings.

Each serving equals:

HE: ½ Bread • ½ Fat • ½ Protein • ¼ Skim Milk •
¾ Slider • 19 Optional Calories

183 Calories • 7 gm Fat • 7 gm Protein • 23 gm Carbohydrate •
506 mg Sodium • 1 gm Fiber

DIABETIC: 1½ Starch *or* Carbohydrate • 1 Fat

Pumpkin Pudding Parfait

☽ Serves 6

1 (4-serving) package JELL-O sugar-free instant butterscotch pudding mix
⅔ cup Carnation Nonfat Dry Milk Powder
1 teaspoon pumpkin pie spice
2 cups (one 16-ounce can) pumpkin
1 cup (one 8-ounce can) crushed pineapple, packed in fruit juice, undrained
¾ cup Cool Whip Lite☆
2 tablespoons (½ ounce) chopped pecans

In a large bowl, combine dry pudding mix, dry milk powder, and pumpkin pie spice. Add pumpkin and undrained pineapple. Mix well using a wire whisk. Blend in ¼ cup Cool Whip Lite. Evenly spoon mixture into 6 parfait or dessert dishes. Top each with 1 tablespoon Cool Whip Lite and 1 teaspoon pecans. Refrigerate for at least 20 minutes.

Each serving equals:

HE: ⅔ Vegetable • ⅓ Fruit • ⅓ Skim Milk • ⅓ Fat • ¼ Slider • 15 Optional Calories

146 Calories • 2 gm Fat • 4 gm Protein • 28 gm Carbohydrate • 273 mg Sodium • 3 gm Fiber

DIABETIC: 1 Starch • 1 Fruit

Layered Chocolate Raspberry Pie

● Serves 8

> 2 (4-serving) packages JELL-O sugar-free instant chocolate pudding mix
>
> 1 (4-serving) package JELL-O sugar-free raspberry gelatin
>
> 1⅓ cups Carnation Nonfat Dry Milk Powder
>
> 2½ cups water
>
> 1 (6-ounce) Keebler chocolate piecrust
>
> ½ cup raspberry spreadable fruit spread
>
> ¾ cup Cool Whip Lite

In a large bowl, combine dry pudding mixes, dry gelatin, dry milk powder, and water. Mix well using a wire whisk. Spread pudding mixture evenly into piecrust. Refrigerate 5 minutes. Evenly spread spreadable fruit over pudding mixture. Spread Cool Whip Lite evenly over top. Refrigerate for at least 20 minutes. Cut into 8 servings.

HINTS: 1. Spreadable fruit spreads best at room temperature.

2. Any compatible gelatin and spreadable fruit combination may be used.

Each serving equals:

HE: 1 Fruit • ½ Bread • ½ Skim Milk • 1 Slider •
19 Optional Calories

238 Calories • 6 gm Fat • 6 gm Protein • 40 gm Carbohydrate •
369 mg Sodium • 1 gm Fiber

DIABETIC: 1½ Starch • 1 Fruit • 1 Fat

Grape Cream Pie

● Serves 8

> 1 (4-serving) package JELL-O sugar-free instant vanilla pudding mix
>
> ⅔ cup Carnation Nonfat Dry Milk Powder
>
> 1¼ cups Diet Rite white grape soda or water
>
> 1 cup (6 ounces) Thompson grapes, sliced
>
> 1 (6-ounce) Keebler shortbread piecrust
>
> ¾ cup Cool Whip Lite
>
> ½ teaspoon coconut extract
>
> 2 tablespoons flaked coconut

In a medium bowl, combine dry pudding mix, dry milk powder, and Diet Rite soda. Mix well using a wire whisk. Stir in grapes. Spread mixture evenly into piecrust. Refrigerate while preparing topping. In a small bowl, combine Cool Whip Lite and coconut extract. Spread topping mixture evenly over pudding mixture. Evenly sprinkle coconut over top. Refrigerate for at least 20 minutes. Cut into 8 servings.

Each serving equals:

HE: ½ Bread • ¼ Fruit • ¼ Skim Milk • 1 Slider •
2 Optional Calories

---

170 Calories • 6 gm Fat • 3 gm Protein • 26 gm Carbohydrate •
300 mg Sodium • 1 gm Fiber

DIABETIC: 1½ Carbohydrate • 1 Fat

Warm Apple Banana Ice Cream Treats

◐ Serves 4

1 cup (1 medium) sliced banana

1 cup (2 small) cored, unpeeled, and diced cooking apples

¼ cup apricot spreadable fruit spread

2 tablespoons (½ ounce) chopped pecans

1 cup Wells' Blue Bunny sugar-free and fat-free vanilla ice cream or any sugar-
and fat-free ice cream

Evenly divide banana and apples among four (6-ounce) custard cups. Spoon 1 tablespoon fruit spread and 1½ teaspoons pecans over top of each. Microwave on HIGH (100% power) for 2 to 3 minutes or until hot. Top each with ¼ cup ice cream. Serve at once.

Each serving equals:

HE: 2 Fruit • ¼ Fat • ¼ Slider • 5 Optional Calories

146 Calories • 2 gm Fat • 2 gm Protein • 30 gm Carbohydrate •
40 mg Sodium • 1 gm Fiber

DIABETIC: 2 Fruit • ½ Fat

Tropical Pleasure Pie

○ Serves 8

1 cup (1 medium) diced banana

1 (6-ounce) Keebler graham cracker piecrust

1 (4-serving) package JELL-O sugar-free instant pistachio pudding mix

⅔ cup Carnation Nonfat Dry Milk Powder

1 cup (one 8-ounce can) crushed pineapple, packed in fruit juice, drained, and ¼ cup liquid reserved

1 cup water

1 cup Cool Whip Lite☆

1 cup (one 11-ounce can) mandarin oranges, rinsed and drained

1 teaspoon coconut extract

2 tablespoons flaked coconut

Layer banana in bottom of piecrust. In a large bowl, combine dry pudding mix and dry milk powder. Add reserved pineapple liquid and water. Mix well using a wire whisk. Blend in ¼ cup Cool Whip Lite. Add pineapple and mandarin oranges. Mix gently to combine. Spread mixture evenly over banana. Refrigerate while preparing topping. In a small bowl, combine remaining ¾ cup Cool Whip Lite and coconut extract. Spread topping mixture evenly over pudding mixture. Evenly sprinkle coconut over top. Refrigerate for at least 20 minutes. Cut into 8 servings.

HINT: To prevent banana from turning brown, mix with 1 teaspoon lemon juice or sprinkle with Fruit Fresh.

Each serving equals:

HE: ¾ Fruit • ½ Bread • ¼ Skim Milk • 1 Slider • 6 Optional Calories

206 Calories • 6 gm Fat • 3 gm Protein • 35 gm Carbohydrate • 331 mg Sodium • 1 gm Fiber

DIABETIC: 1 Fruit • 1 Starch • 1 Fat

Hawaiian Pudding Dessert

● Serves 8

12 (2½ inch) graham cracker squares☆

1 (4-serving) package JELL-O sugar-free instant vanilla pudding mix

⅔ cup Carnation Nonfat Dry Milk Powder

1 cup (one 8-ounce can) crushed pineapple, packed in fruit juice, undrained

½ cup water

1 cup (1 medium) diced banana

1 cup Cool Whip Lite

1 teaspoon coconut extract

2 tablespoons (½ ounce) chopped pecans

2 tablespoons flaked coconut

4 maraschino cherries, halved

Evenly arrange 9 of the graham crackers in a 9-by-9-inch cake pan. In a large bowl, combine dry pudding mix, dry milk powder, undrained pineapple, and water. Mix well using a wire whisk. Fold in banana. Evenly spread mixture over graham crackers. In a small bowl, combine Cool Whip Lite and coconut extract. Spread topping mixture evenly over pudding mixture. Crush remaining 3 graham crackers. In a small bowl, combine cracker crumbs, pecans, and coconut. Evenly sprinkle crumb mixture over top. Garnish with cherry halves. Refrigerate for at least 20 minutes. Cut into 8 servings.

HINT: To prevent banana from turning brown, mix with 1 teaspoon lemon juice or sprinkle with Fruit Fresh.

Each serving equals:

HE: ½ Bread • ½ Fruit • ¼ Skim Milk • ¼ Fat • ½ Slider • 1 Optional Calorie

147 Calories • 3 gm Fat • 3 gm Protein • 27 gm Carbohydrate • 267 mg Sodium • 1 gm Fiber

DIABETIC: 1 Starch • 1 Fat • ½ Fruit

Apricot-Pecan Tarts

❍ Serves 6

1 (4-serving) package JELL-O sugar-free instant vanilla pudding mix

⅔ cup Carnation Nonfat Dry Milk Powder

1⅓ cups water

6 tablespoons apricot spreadable fruit spread

3 tablespoons (¾ ounce) chopped pecans

1 (6-single serve) package Keebler graham cracker crusts

6 tablespoons Cool Whip Lite

In a medium bowl, combine dry pudding mix, dry milk powder, and water. Mix well using a wire whisk. Blend in apricot spreadable fruit and pecans. Evenly spoon mixture into crusts. Top each with 1 tablespoon Cool Whip Lite. Refrigerate for at least 20 minutes.

Each serving equals:

HE: 1 Fruit • ¾ Fat • ½ Bread • ⅓ Skim Milk • ¾ Slider • 17 Optional Calories

240 Calories • 8 gm Fat • 4 gm Protein • 38 gm Carbohydrate • 456 mg Sodium • 1 gm Fiber

DIABETIC: 1½ Starch • 1 Fat *or* 1½ Carbohydrate • 1 Fat • 1 Fruit

Cherry Cola Cheesecake

● Serves 8

2 (8-ounce)-packages Philadelphia fat-free cream cheese

1 (4-serving) package JELL-O sugar-free instant vanilla pudding mix

⅔ cup Carnation Nonfat Dry Milk Powder

1 cup Diet Coke

¾ cup Cool Whip Lite☆

1 (6-ounce) Keebler graham cracker piecrust

½ cup cherry spreadable fruit spread

2 tablespoons (½ ounce) chopped pecans

In a large bowl, stir cream cheese with a spoon until soft. Add dry pudding mix, dry milk powder, and Diet Coke. Mix well using a wire whisk. Blend in ¼ cup Cool Whip Lite. Spread mixture evenly into piecrust. In a small bowl, combine remaining ½ cup Cool Whip Lite and cherry spreadable fruit. Spread topping mixture evenly over set filling. Evenly sprinkle pecans over top. Refrigerate for at least 20 minutes. Cut into 8 servings.

HINT: Spreadable fruit spreads best at room temperature.

Each serving equals:

HE: 1 Protein • 1 Fruit • ½ Bread • ¼ Skim Milk • ¼ Fat • ¾ Slider • 18 Optional Calories

251 Calories • 7 gm Fat • 11 gm Protein • 36 gm Carbohydrate • 686 mg Sodium • 0 gm Fiber

DIABETIC: 1 Meat • 1 Fruit • 1 Starch • 1 Fat

Lemon Orange Ade

● Serves 8 (1 cup)

1 tub Crystal Light sugar-free lemonade mix
8 cups water
¼ of an orange cut into chunks, including skin and seeds

In a large pitcher, combine dry lemonade mix and water. Mix well using a long spoon. Pour 2 cups of prepared lemonade into blender; add orange chunks and blend on HIGH for 30 to 45 seconds. Pour back into the pitcher of lemonade mixture and mix well. Serve over ice.

Each serving equals:

HE: 1 Optional Calorie

0 Calories • 0 gm Fat • 0 gm Protein • 0 gm Carbohydrate •
0 mg Sodium • 0 gm Fiber

DIABETIC: Free Food

Heavenly Orange Fluff

● Serves 6

¾ cup Yoplait plain fat-free yogurt

1 cup Carnation Nonfat Dry Milk Powder☆

Sugar substitute to equal 2 tablespoons sugar

1 teaspoon coconut extract

¾ cup Cool Whip Lite

1 (4-serving) package JELL-O sugar-free orange gelatin

1 (4-serving) package JELL-O sugar-free instant vanilla pudding mix

1 cup Diet Mountain Dew

1 cup (one 8-ounce can) crushed pineapple, packed in fruit juice, undrained

1 cup (one 11-ounce can) mandarin oranges, rinsed and drained

2 tablespoons flaked coconut

In a small bowl, combine yogurt and ⅓ cup dry milk powder. Add sugar substitute and coconut extract. Mix well to combine. Stir in Cool Whip Lite. Set aside. In a large bowl, combine dry gelatin, dry pudding mix, and remaining ⅔ cup dry milk powder. Add Diet Mountain Dew and undrained pineapple. Mix well using a wire whisk. Fold yogurt mixture into pudding mixture. Add mandarin oranges. Mix gently to combine. Evenly spoon mixture into 6 dessert dishes. Top each with 1 teaspoon coconut. Refrigerate for at least 20 minutes.

HINT: Diet 7-UP or water may be used in place of Diet Mountain Dew.

Each serving equals:

HE: ⅔ Fruit • ⅔ Skim Milk • ½ Slider • 10 Optional Calories

141 Calories • 1 gm Fat • 7 gm Protein • 26 gm Carbohydrate • 353 mg Sodium • 0 gm Fiber

DIABETIC: 1 Fruit • 1 Skim Milk

Apple-Cranberry Cider

● Serves 4 (1 cup)

1½ cups unsweetened apple juice
1¾ cups Diet 7-UP
1 cup Ocean Spray reduced-calorie cranberry juice cocktail
1 teaspoon apple pie spice

In a medium saucepan, combine apple juice, Diet 7-UP, and cranberry juice. Add apple pie spice. Mix well to combine. Simmer for 15 minutes, stirring occasionally.

Each serving equals:

HE: 1 Fruit

56 Calories • 0 gm Fat • 0 gm Protein • 14 gm Carbohydrate • 29 mg Sodium • 0 gm Fiber

DIABETIC: 1 Fruit

Queen Anne's Cheesecake

● Serves 8

2 (8-ounce)-packages Philadelphia fat-free cream cheese

1 (4-serving) package JELL-O sugar-free instant vanilla pudding mix

1 (4-serving) package JELL-O sugar-free cherry gelatin

⅔ cup Carnation Nonfat Dry Milk Powder

1 cup (one 8-ounce can) crushed pineapple, packed in fruit juice, undrained

¼ cup water

8 maraschino cherries, quartered

¾ cup Cool Whip Lite☆

1 (6-ounce) Keebler graham cracker piecrust

In a large bowl, stir cream cheese with a spoon until soft. Add dry pudding mix, dry gelatin, dry milk powder, undrained pineapple, and water. Mix well using a wire whisk. Reserve 8 cherry pieces. Gently fold remaining cherry pieces and ¼ cup Cool Whip Lite into pudding mixture. Spread mixture evenly into piecrust. Refrigerate for at least 20 minutes. Cut into 8 servings. When serving, top each piece with 1 tablespoon Cool Whip Lite and garnish with 1 piece of reserved cherry.

Each serving equals:

HE: 1 Protein • ½ Bread • ¼ Fruit • ¼ Skim Milk • 1 Slider •
13 Optional Calories

226 Calories • 6 gm Fat • 12 gm Protein • 31 gm Carbohydrate •
698 mg Sodium • 1 gm Fiber

DIABETIC: 2 Starch *or* Carbohydrate • 1 Meat • 1 Fat

Strawberry Lover's Pudding Treats

● Serves 4

1 (4-serving) package JELL-O sugar-free instant vanilla pudding mix
1 (4-serving) package JELL-O sugar-free strawberry gelatin
⅔ cup Carnation Nonfat Dry Milk Powder
1 cup sliced fresh strawberries, mashed
¾ cup water
½ teaspoon vanilla extract
¼ cup Cool Whip Lite

In a medium bowl, combine dry pudding mix, dry gelatin, and dry milk powder. Add mashed strawberries and water. Mix well using a wire whisk. Blend in vanilla extract and Cool Whip Lite. Evenly spoon mixture into 4 dessert dishes. Refrigerate for at least 20 minutes.

Each serving equals:

HE: ½ Skim Milk • ¼ Fruit • ½ Slider • 5 Optional Calories

93 Calories • 1 gm Fat • 5 gm Protein • 16 gm Carbohydrate • 446 mg Sodium • 0 gm Fiber

DIABETIC: 1 Starch *or* Carbohydrate

Fudgy Peanut Butter Brownies

Using applesauce in place of shortening when you're baking produces a wonderfully moist treat, especially in this recipe that sparkles with peanut butter and chocolate flavors! ❤ Serves 8 (2 each)

1½ cups Bisquick Reduced Fat Baking Mix

1 (4-serving) package JELL-O sugar-free instant chocolate fudge pudding mix

½ cup creamy Peter Pan reduced-fat peanut butter

1 cup unsweetened applesauce

1 teaspoon vanilla extract

2 eggs or equivalent in egg substitute

Preheat oven to 350 degrees. Spray a 11-by-7-inch baking pan with butter-flavored cooking spray. In a large bowl, combine baking mix and dry pudding mix. Add peanut butter, applesauce, vanilla extract, and eggs. Mix well to combine. Spread batter into prepared baking pan. Bake for 20 to 25 minutes. Place baking pan on a wire rack and allow to cool completely. Cut into 16 bars.

Each serving equals:

HE: 1¼ Protein (¼ limited) • 1 Bread • 1 Fat • ¼ Fruit •
18 Optional Calories

229 Calories • 8 gm Fat • 7 gm Protein • 30 gm Carbohydrate •
518 mg Sodium • 25 mg Calcium • 2 gm Fiber

DIABETIC: 2 Starch/Carbohydrate • 1 Meat • ½ Fat

Uptown Strawberry-Chocolate Cheesecake

I never get tired of creating wonderful desserts that feature fresh strawberries, but this one is particularly special. Maybe it's the almonds, or perhaps the chocolate syrup, but this is one fruit pie you'll want to serve again and again.

◐ Serves 8

> 2 (8-ounce) packages Philadelphia fat-free cream cheese
>
> 1 (4-serving) package JELL-O sugar-free instant white chocolate pudding mix
>
> ⅔ cup Carnation Nonfat Dry Milk Powder
>
> 1 cup water
>
> ¼ cup Cool Whip Free
>
> ½ teaspoon almond extract
>
> 1 (6-ounce) Keebler chocolate piecrust
>
> 2 cups chopped fresh strawberries
>
> ¼ cup (1 ounce) sliced almonds
>
> 2 tablespoons Hershey's Lite Chocolate Syrup

In a large bowl, stir cream cheese with a spoon until soft. Add dry pudding mix, dry milk powder, and water. Mix well using a wire whisk. Blend in Cool Whip Free and almond extract. Evenly spread mixture into piecrust. Sprinkle strawberries and almonds over cheesecake filling. Cover and refrigerate for at least 30 minutes. Just before serving, drizzle chocolate syrup over top. Cut into 8 servings.

Each serving equals:

> HE: 1 Protein • ¼ Fruit • ¼ Fat • ¼ Skim Milk • 1 Slider • 5 Optional Calories
> _____
> 231 Calories • 7 gm Fat • 12 gm Protein • 30 gm Carbohydrate • 642 mg Sodium • 84 mg Calcium • 2 gm Fiber
> _____
> DIABETIC: 1½ Starch/Carbohydrate • 1 Meat • 1 Fat

This and That

Breakfast from a box might be "instant" when you're in a hurry, but what're just a few moments more in the great scheme of things? I'll tell you: by stirring up something speedy and special like my Pineapple Maple Upside-Down Biscuits, you can still get to work on time, but you've made a memory to last forever in the hearts of your family. That's true of such tasty treats as Rise and Shine French Toast, or a sparkling liquid sensation like my Celebration "Champagne." Instead of watching the clock, you'll be sharing smiles around the table!

Breakfast Fruit Turnovers

No time in the morning, but you want to grab a little something on your way out the door? There are so many terrific flavors in spreadable fruit, you can choose from a smorgasbord of tastes! ☻ Serves 10

1 (10-ounce) can Pillsbury refrigerated buttermilk biscuits
10 teaspoons spreadable fruit (any flavor)

Preheat oven to 425 degrees. Spray a 10-by-15-inch baking sheet with butter-flavored cooking spray. Separate biscuits and roll each biscuit into a 5-inch circle. Place 1 teaspoon spreadable fruit in center of each. Fold biscuit in half and seal edges closed with the tines of a fork. Place biscuits on prepared baking sheet. Lightly spray tops with butter-flavored cooking spray. Bake for 7 to 9 minutes or until golden brown. Serve at once.

Each serving equals:

HE: 1 Bread • ⅓ Fruit

85 Calories • 1 gm Fat • 2 gm Protein • 17 gm Carbohydrate • 243 mg Sodium • 0 mg Calcium • 1 gm Fiber

DIABETIC: 1 Starch

Pineapple-Maple Upside-Down Biscuits

This is a fun surprise to serve at breakfast or even for an after-school snack. Isn't it great to use your microwave for more than reheating coffee? ☻ Serves 6

1 tablespoon reduced-calorie margarine

¼ cup Brown Sugar Twin

1 tablespoon Cary's Sugar Free Maple Syrup

1 cup (one 8-ounce can) sliced pineapple, packed in fruit juice, drained

1 (7.5-ounce) can Pillsbury refrigerated biscuits

In an 8-inch round glass pie plate, melt margarine in microwave. Stir in Brown Sugar Twin and maple syrup. Arrange pineapple slices in mixture, breaking as necessary to fit. Separate biscuits and arrange evenly over pineapple slices. Cover and microwave on HIGH (100% power) for 4 minutes, turning pie plate after 3 minutes. Remove covering and lightly spray top of biscuits with butter-flavored cooking spray. Place serving plate over top of pie plate and invert biscuits onto serving plate. Let set 2 to 3 minutes. Cut into 6 wedges.

Each serving equals:

HE: 1¼ Bread • ⅓ Fruit • ¼ Fat • 5 Optional Calories

117 Calories • 1 gm Fat • 3 gm Protein • 24 gm Carbohydrate •
319 mg Sodium • 6 mg Calcium • 2 gm Fiber

DIABETIC: 1½ Starch/Carbohydrate

Banana Raisin Breakfast Scones

Even if you never bake, you'll find that these are simple to make and oh-so-tasty! They're just perfect for a weekend brunch and fill your kitchen with a luscious aroma.　　❍　　Serves 6

> 1 cup + 2 tablespoons Bisquick Reduced Fat Baking Mix
> ¼ cup Sugar Twin or Sprinkle Sweet
> ¾ teaspoon apple pie spice
> ½ cup raisins
> ⅓ cup (1 ripe medium) mashed banana
> ¼ cup Land O Lake no-fat sour cream
> ½ cup water

Preheat oven to 410 degrees. Spray a 6-hole muffin pan with butter-flavored cooking spray. In a large bowl, combine baking mix, Sugar Twin, apple pie spice, and raisins. Add banana, sour cream, and water. Mix well to combine. Fill prepared muffin wells with batter. Bake for 15 to 18 minutes. Place muffin pan on a wire rack and let set for 5 minutes. Remove scones from pan and continue cooling on wire rack.

Each serving equals:

HE: 1 Fruit • 1 Bread • 14 Optional Calories

---

137 Calories • 1 gm Fat • 3 gm Protein • 29 gm Carbohydrate • 276 mg Sodium • 35 mg Calcium • 1 gm Fiber

---

DIABETIC: 1 Fruit • 1 Starch/Carbohydrate

Rise-and-Shine French Toast

I like to think of this breakfast treat as a "meal-in-a-slice"! You get your orange juice, your egg, and of course, your slice of bread—such an efficient way to eat healthy! What better way to say "Good Morning!"   ☻   Serves 2

2 eggs or equivalent in egg substitute
½ cup unsweetened orange juice
½ teaspoon ground cinnamon
4 slices reduced-calorie bread

In a shallow bowl, combine eggs, orange juice, and cinnamon. Beat well using a fork. Dip bread slices into mixture, being sure to coat both sides. Place bread slices on griddle or large skillet sprayed with butter-flavored cooking spray. Cook for 3 to 4 minutes on each side or until golden brown. Serve at once.

Each serving equals:

HE: 1 Protein (limited) • 1 Bread • ½ Fruit

198 Calories • 6 gm Fat • 11 gm Protein • 25 gm Carbohydrate • 294 mg Sodium • 71 mg Calcium • 5 gm Fiber

DIABETIC: 1 Meat • 1 Starch • ½ Fruit

Apple Pie Flapjacks

My grandbabies, Josh and Zach, just love pancakes, so while I don't often make them when it's just Cliff and me, I enjoy getting up to prepare a dish like this when the boys are visiting. Their smiles when I serve these flapjacks are just irresistible.

○ Serves 4 (2 pancakes)

> *1½ cups Aunt Jemima Reduced Calorie Pancake Mix*
> *½ teaspoon apple pie spice*
> *1⅓ cups water*
> *1 cup (2 small) finely chopped unpeeled cooking apples*

In a medium bowl, combine pancake mix and apple pie spice. Add water. Mix well to combine. Stir in apples. Using a ¼-cup measuring cup as a guide, pour batter onto a griddle or large skillet sprayed with butter-flavored cooking spray, forming 8 pancakes. Cook over medium heat about 3 minutes on each side or until golden brown.

HINTS: 1. Great served with warmed Cary's Sugar Free Maple Syrup or apple butter.
2. Also good with 2 tablespoons chopped pecans stirred into batter with apples.

Each serving equals:

HE: 2 Bread • ½ Fruit

197 Calories • 1 gm Fat • 9 gm Protein • 38 gm Carbohydrate • 580 mg Sodium • 275 mg Calcium • 6 gm Fiber

DIABETIC: 2 Starch/Carbohydrate • ½ Fruit

Hacienda Eggs

Here's my version of that Mexican classic, huevos rancheros—a fiesta of flavors that gets your day off to a great start! Even if you love spicy food, experiment to discover whether you still "like it hot" first thing in the morning!

♥ Serves 4

4 eggs or equivalent in egg substitute

½ teaspoon lemon pepper

4 slices reduced-calorie bread, toasted and cubed

⅓ cup (1½ ounces) shredded Kraft reduced-fat Cheddar cheese

½ cup chunky salsa (mild, medium, or hot)

¼ cup Land O Lakes no-fat sour cream

In a medium bowl, combine eggs and lemon pepper using a wire whisk. Place toast cubes in a large skillet sprayed with butter-flavored cooking spray. Pour eggs over toast. Cook over medium heat until eggs begin to set, stirring occasionally. Sprinkle Cheddar cheese evenly over the top. Cover, remove from heat, and let set for 2 to 3 minutes or until cheese melts. Cut into 4 servings. When serving, top each piece with 2 tablespoons salsa and 1 tablespoon sour cream.

Each serving equals:

HE: 1½ Protein (1 limited) • ½ Bread • ¼ Vegetable •
15 Optional Calories

163 Calories • 7 gm Fat • 12 gm Protein • 13 gm Carbohydrate •
394 mg Sodium • 165 mg Calcium • 3 gm Fiber

DIABETIC: 1 Meat • 1 Starch • ½ Vegetable

Spanish Potato Chips

Packaged potato chips "pack" a real wallop when it comes to calories and fat, so they're not a particularly good choice if eating healthy is your goal. Instead, slice your potatoes as thin as you can, cook up a batch of these, and then stand back—as your friends and family gobble them down quicker than the eye can see!

◑ Serves 4 (½ cup)

> *2 cups (10 ounces) thinly sliced raw unpeeled potatoes*
> *¼ teaspoon salt*
> *1 teaspoon chili seasoning*

Arrange potato slices in a single layer circle on a microwave bacon-cooking rack sprayed with butter-flavored cooking spray. Sprinkle with salt and chili seasoning. Microwave on HIGH (100% power) for 5 to 7 minutes or until browned. Turn halfway through cooking time. Let set for 1 minute.

HINTS: 1. If using Cuisinart blade, use #1.
                 2. If using a conventional oven, place potato slices on a baking sheet sprayed with butter-flavored cooking spray and bake at 400 degrees for about 20 minutes.

Each serving equals:

HE: ½ Bread

40 Calories • 0 gm Fat • 1 gm Protein • 9 gm Carbohydrate • 137 mg Sodium • 5 mg Calcium • 1 gm Fiber

DIABETIC: ½ Starch

Nutty "Candy" Treats

These little goodies are incredibly tasty, and I give you a "real-life" serving—four of them! You see, if you only got to have one, you'd be inclined to sneak a few more and feel bad about it, but that's no way to live. Enjoy every bite!

☻ Serves 6 (4 each)

> 2 tablespoons chunky Peter Pan reduced-fat peanut butter
> ¼ cup Cary's Sugar Free Maple Syrup
> ¼ cup Sugar Twin or Sprinkle Sweet
> ⅔ cup Carnation Nonfat Dry Milk Powder
> 1 cup (3 ounces) quick oats
> ¼ cup (1 ounce) chopped unsalted dry roasted peanuts

In a medium bowl, combine peanut butter, maple syrup, Sugar Twin, and dry milk powder. Stir in oats and peanuts. Place waxed paper on a cookie sheet. Drop mixture by teaspoonfuls to form 24 treats. Refrigerate for at least 20 minutes. Cover and refrigerate leftovers.

Each serving equals:

HE: 1 Fat • ⅔ Bread • ½ Protein • ⅓ Skim Milk •
11 Optional Calories

166 Calories • 6 gm Fat • 8 gm Protein • 20 gm Carbohydrate •
90 mg Sodium • 104 mg Calcium • 2 gm Fiber

DIABETIC: 1½ Starch/Carbohydrate • 1 Fat

Fast-Food Hamburger Sauce

You know the one I mean—that secret sauce that tops those all-beef patties . . .
Here's my take on this mysterious blend, which does make your everyday burger
a little more special!   ❍   Makes about 1½ cups

1 cup Kraft fat-free mayonnaise
⅓ cup Kraft Fat Free French Dressing
¼ cup sweet pickle relish
¼ teaspoon black pepper
1 tablespoon dried onion flakes

In a medium bowl, combine mayonnaise and French dressing. Add pickle
relish, black pepper, and onion flakes. Mix well to combine. Cover and refrigerate
at least 15 minutes.

Each 1 tablespoon serving equals:

HE: 16 Optional Calories

16 Calories • 0 gm Fat • 0 gm Protein • 4 gm Carbohydrate •
138 mg Sodium • 1 mg Calcium • 0 gm Fiber

DIABETIC: 1 Free Food

Maple Peanut Butter Dressing

Why not take a different approach the next time you serve a beautiful and healthy fruit salad? This "nutty" dressing is delightfully tasty—the perfect foil to the sweetness of ripe, ripe fruit! ☻ Serves 8 (2 tablespoons)

½ *cup Kraft fat-free mayonnaise*
¼ *cup Cary's Sugar Free Maple Syrup*
¼ *cup Peter Pan reduced-fat peanut butter*

In a medium bowl, combine mayonnaise and maple syrup. Add peanut butter. Mix well using a wire whisk. Cover and refrigerate for at least 20 minutes.

HINT: Wonderful on a fruit salad.

Each serving equals:

HE: ½ Protein • ½ Fat • 15 Optional Calories

63 Calories • 3 gm Fat • 2 gm Protein • 7 gm Carbohydrate • 184 mg Sodium • 0 mg Calcium • 0 gm Fiber

DIABETIC: ½ Starch/Carbohydrate • ½ Fat

Hawaiian Fruit Dip

Served with a tray of sliced fresh pineapple or whole strawberries, this is a truly scrumptious way to welcome guests to a brunch or lunch party! If it's very hot out, you might want to serve half of it at the start, then replace the dish with a fresh one after the dip starts to get warm.   ☻   Serves 6 (⅓ cup)

¾ cup Yoplait plain fat-free yogurt

⅓ cup Carnation Nonfat Dry Milk Powder

½ cup orange marmalade spreadable fruit

1 cup (one 8-ounce can) crushed pineapple, packed in fruit juice, well drained

1 teaspoon coconut extract

½ cup Cool Whip Free

In a medium bowl, combine yogurt and dry milk powder. Blend in spreadable fruit. Add pineapple, coconut extract, and Cool Whip Free. Mix gently to combine. Cover and refrigerate for at least 30 minutes. Gently stir again just before serving.

HINT: Wonderful with fresh pineapple chunks and whole fresh strawberries.

Each serving equals:

HE: 1¼ Fruit • ¼ Skim Milk • 10 optional calories

68 Calories • 0 gm Fat • 4 gm Protein • 13 gm Carbohydrate •
32 mg Sodium • 81 mg Calcium • 0 gm Fiber

DIABETIC: 1 Fruit • ½ Starch/Carbohydrate

Cranapple Dew

Looking for a refreshing beverage to serve as a change from lemonade? Try this sparkling combo of cranberry and lemon, and you may find yourself serving it all the time!　　❂　　Serves 4 (full ¾ cup)

2 cups Ocean Spray reduced-calorie cranapple drink
1 cup Diet Mountain Dew
1 cup ice cubes
Lemon wedges (optional)

In a blender container, combine cranapple drink and Diet Mountain Dew. Add ice cubes. Cover and process on BLEND until smooth. When serving, garnish each glass with lemon wedge, if desired.

Each serving equals:

HE: ½ Fruit

24 Calories • 0 gm Fat • 0 gm Protein • 6 gm Carbohydrate • 24 mg Sodium • 0 mg Calcium • 0 gm Fiber

DIABETIC: ½ Fruit

Celebration "Champagne"

Every festive occasion needs a few sparkling drinks, and these days, many people opt for the nonalcoholic kind. This bubbly apple-juice blend looks like the "real thing" and tastes even better!   ☻   Serves 6 (1 cup)

3 cups cold unsweetened apple juice
3 cups cold Diet 7-UP
6 maraschino cherries

In a large pitcher, combine apple juice and Diet 7-UP. Refrigerate for at least 30 minutes. When serving, pour into champagne glasses and garnish each glass with a maraschino cherry.

Each serving equals:

HE: 1 Fruit • 10 Optional Calories

68 Calories • 0 gm Fat • 0 gm Protein • 17 gm Carbohydrate •
16 mg Sodium • 12 mg Calcium • 0 gm Fiber

DIABETIC: 1 Fruit

Making Healthy Exchanges Work for You

You're ready now to begin a wonderful journey to better health. In the preceding pages, you've discovered the remarkable variety of good food available to you when you begin eating the Healthy Exchanges way. You've stocked your pantry and learned many of my food preparation "secrets" that will point you on the way to delicious success.

But before I let you go, I'd like to share a few tips that I've learned while traveling toward healthier eating habits. It took me a long time to learn how to eat *smarter*. In fact, I'm still working on it. But I am getting better. For years, I could *inhale* a five-course meal in five minutes flat—and still make room for a second helping of dessert.

Now I follow certain signposts on the road that help me stay on the right path. I hope these ideas will help point you in the right direction as well.

1. **Eat slowly** so your brain has time to catch up with your tummy. Cut and chew each bite slowly. Try putting your fork down between bites. Stop eating as soon as you feel full. Crumple your napkin and throw it on top of your plate so you don't continue to eat when you are no longer hungry.

2. **Smaller plates** may help you feel more satisfied by your food portions *and* limit the amount you can put on the plate.

3. **Watch portion size.** If you are *truly* hungry, you can always add more food to your plate once you've finished your initial serving. But remember to count the additional food accordingly.

4. **Always eat at your dining-room or kitchen table.** You deserve better than nibbling from an open refrigerator or over the sink. Make an attractive place setting, even if you're eating alone. Feed your eyes as well as your stomach. By always eating at a table, you will become much more aware of your true food intake. For some reason, many of us conveniently "forget" the food we swallow while standing over the stove or munching in the car or on the run.

5. **Avoid doing anything else while you are eating.** If you read the paper or watch television while you eat, it's easy to consume too much food without realizing it, because you are concentrating on something else besides what you're eating. Then, when you look down at your plate and see that it's empty, you wonder where all the food went and why you still feel hungry.

Day by day, as you travel the path to good health, it will become easier to make the right choices, to eat smarter. But don't ever fool yourself into thinking that you'll be able to put your eating habits on cruise control and forget about them. Making a commitment to eat good healthy food and sticking to it takes some effort. But with all the good-tasting recipes in this Healthy Exchanges cookbook, just think how well you're going to eat— and enjoy it—from now on!

Healthy Lean Bon Appetit!

Index of Recipes